# California Wine Country Restaurants

# 2009

**LOCAL EDITOR**
Meesha Halm

**STAFF EDITOR**
Cynthia Kilian

Published and distributed by
Zagat Survey, LLC
4 Columbus Circle
New York, NY 10019
T: 212.977.6000
E: californiawine@zagat.com
www.zagat.com

## ACKNOWLEDGMENTS

We thank Jon, Olive and Jude Fox, Sharron Wood and Steven Shukow, as well as the following members of our staff: Christina Livadiotis (assistant editor), Amy Cao (editorial assistant), Sean Beachell, Maryanne Bertollo, Sandy Cheng, Reni Chin, Larry Cohn, Bill Corsello, Deirdre Donovan, Alison Flick, Jeff Freier, Sharon Gintzler, Justin Hartung, Roy Jacob, Natalie Lebert, Mike Liao, Allison Lynn, Dave Makulec, Chris Miragliotta, Andre Pilette, Josh Rogers, Becky Ruthenburg, Aleksandra Shander, Donna Marino Wilkins, Liz Borod Wright, Yoji Yamaguchi, Sharon Yates, Anna Zappia and Kyle Zolner.


ISBN-13: 978-1-57006-999-4
ISBN-10: 1-57006-999-9
Printed in the
United States of America

# What's New

It's been a vintage year for the Wine Country with the top restaurants in the San Francisco Bay Area Survey proving to be outside the city proper and in among the vine lands. For the first time since ceding the No. 1 Food spot in 2003 to Gary Danko, Thomas Keller's Napa mecca, **The French Laundry,** has returned once more to the top, while Sonoma's haute **Cyrus** has taken over the No. 2 spot.

**MOTORING TO MENDOCINO:** Overall, the number of Wine Country restaurants rating a Food score of 26 or higher tallied in at 15, up from nine last year. This may explain why 30% of our surveyors say they'd travel an hour for a great dinner, while another 22% would drive over an hour.

**NAPA RIVER RISING:** Downtown Napa is making waves along its riverfront promenade with the opening of the Oxbow Public Market, which houses, among others, newcomers **Folio Enoteca & Winery** from Michael Mondavi and **Oxbow Wine Merchant,** with a branch of **Hog Island Oyster Co.** on its way. Relocating from Rutherford, chef Ken Frank's truffle-centric **La Toque** plans a press-time premiere in the luxurious new Westin Verasa just blocks away from COPIA, the cultural center for food, wine and the arts.

**SONOMA SHIFTS:** Co-owners Doug Keane and Nick Peyton of Cyrus continue to expand their fine-dining options with a new off-site private dining service, but they've also stepped into the casual arena by taking over longtime locals' favorite **Healdsburg Bar & Grill.** Bodega Bay bid adieu to the quirky, beloved Seaweed Café, and in Santa Rosa, executive chef Jeffrey Madura exited **John Ash & Co.** after 20 years at the helm of that pioneering Wine Country restaurant. But the sleepy town of Windsor woke up its dining scene with the arrival of NYC-transplant Rudy Mihal's **Odyssey.**

September 23, 2008 — Meesha Halm

# Top Food Ratings

Excludes places with low votes.

**29** French Laundry | *Amer./French*
Cyrus | *French*

**27** Redd Restaurant | *Californian*

**26** Meadowood Rest. | *Cal.*
Ad Hoc | *American*
Bistro Jeanty | *French*
Terra | *American*
Hana Japanese | *Japanese*
Cafe La Haye | *Amer./Cal.*
Martini House | *American*
La Toque | *French*
Madrona Manor | *Amer./Fr.*
Bouchon | *French*
Farmhouse Inn | *Californian*
Bistro des Copains | *French*

**25** Della Fattoria | *Bakery/Eclectic*
Syrah | *Californian/French*
Mirepoix | *French*
Étoile | *Californian*
Willi's Wine Bar | *Eclectic*
Auberge du Soleil | *Cal./French*
Cafe Beaujolais | *Cal./French*
Farm | *American*

**24** Ubuntu | *Californian/Vegan*
Cook St. Helena | *Italian*
Mustards Grill | *Amer./Cal.*
K&L Bistro | *French*
Celadon | *American/Eclectic*
Cole's Chop House | *Steak*
Annalien | *Vietnamese*
Cucina Paradiso | *Italian*
zazu | *American/Italian*
Applewood Inn | *Californian*
Dry Creek Kitchen | *Amer.*
Santi | *Italian*
Zuzu | *Spanish*
Cindy's Backstreet | *Amer./Cal.*

**23** Go Fish | *Eclectic/Seafood*
Julia's Kitchen | *Cal./French*
Willow Wood | *Eclectic/Med.*
fig cafe & winebar | *French*
Tra Vigne | *Italian*
Azzurro Pizzeria | *Pizza*
Rutherford Grill | *American*
girl & the fig | *French*
Willi's Seafood | *Seafood*
Bistro Don Giovanni | *Italian*
MacCallum House* | *Cal.*
Central Market | *Cal./Med.*
John Ash & Co. | *Californian*

* Indicates a tie with restaurant above

# Napa County Top Food

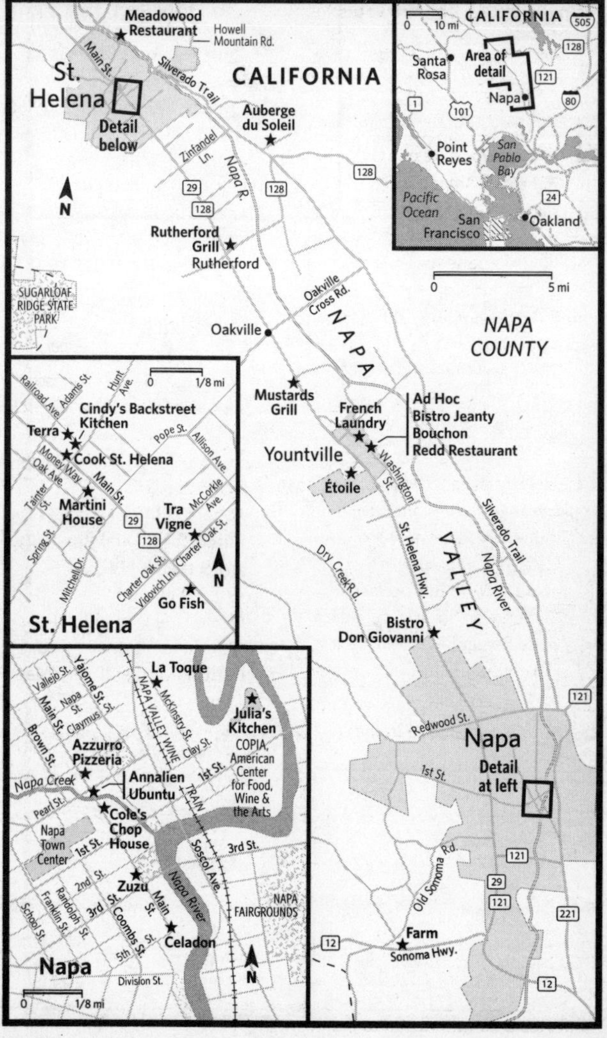

# Sonoma County & North Top Food

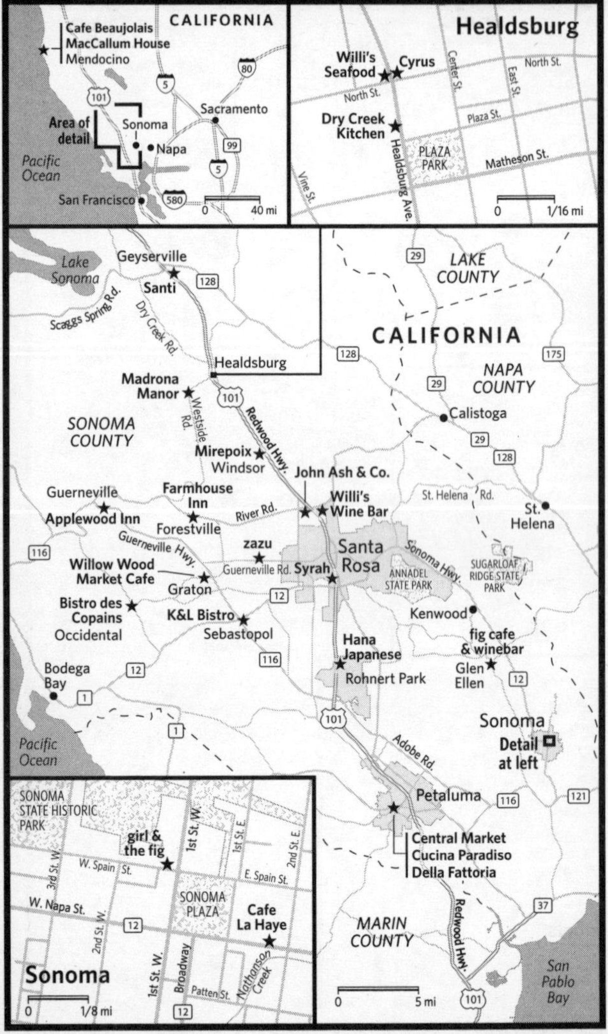

# Ratings & Symbols

Zagat Top Spot | Name | Symbols | Cuisine | Zagat Ratings: FOOD, DECOR, SERVICE, COST

**Area, Address & Contact**

**Review, surveyor comments in quotes**

| | | FOOD | DECOR | SERVICE | COST |
|---|---|---|---|---|---|
| Z **Tim & Nina's** ◐ *Californian* | ▽ | 23 | 9 | 13 | $15 |

**Calistoga** | 9999 Lincoln Ave. (Washington St.) | 707-555-1234 | www.zagat.com

Open "when T and N sober up", this Calistoga cafe-cum-wine bar offers "real Cal cuisine" ("it's picked outside the back door"), and the wine comes straight "from their bathtub"; it all tastes "surprisingly good" and is "dirt-cheap" – that is, if you can ever get served by the "tippling waiters."

**Ratings** **Food, Decor** and **Service** are rated on the Zagat 0 to 30 scale.

0 - 9 poor to fair

10 - 15 fair to good

16 - 19 good to very good

20 - 25 very good to excellent

26 - 30 extraordinary to perfection

▽ low response | less reliable

**Cost** Reflects our surveyors' average estimate of the price of a dinner with one drink and tip and is a benchmark only. Lunch is usually 25% less. Costs for prix fixe-only places reflect the lowest-priced menu plus 30%. For **newcomers** or survey **write-ins** listed without ratings, the price range is indicated as follows:

I $25 and below

M $26 to $40

E $41 to $65

VE $66 or more

**Symbols**

Z Zagat Top Spot (highest Food rated)

◐ serves after 11 PM

Ⓢ closed on Sunday

Ⓜ closed on Monday

⊄ no credit cards accepted

| | FOOD | DECOR | SERVICE | COST |
|---|---|---|---|---|
| Ad Hoc | 26 | 19 | 24 | $62 |
| Albion River Inn | 22 | 24 | 23 | $51 |
| Alexis Baking Company | 22 | 11 | 14 | $17 |
| All Seasons Bistro | ∇ 21 | 15 | 18 | $37 |

**Z Ad Hoc** *American* 26 | 19 | 24 | $62

**Yountville** | 6476 Washington St. (bet. California Dr. & Oak Circle) | 707-944-2487 | www.adhocrestaurant.com

"Thomas Keller goes downscale - deliciously" - "bringing the same care and flavors" to Traditional American "comfort food served family-style" at his "French Laundry for the masses"; this "unpretentious" "diner" hawks the "perfect wine country casual dinner" - and it's always "bustling with locals and the friendliest service in Yountville"; true, the set nightly prix fixe four-course affair "isn't for control freaks", but heck, it's "all good", and it "doesn't 'ad' up to a high bill."

**Albion River Inn** *Californian* 22 | 24 | 23 | $51

**Albion** | 3790 N. Hwy. 1 (Spring Grove Rd.) | 707-937-1919 | www.albionriverinn.com

"What a site!" swoon smitten sojourners who think they're "California Dreamin'" when they visit this "gorgeous" Albion dinner house on an "ocean bluff" with a "lovely lawn to stroll between courses", live piano music and a fireplace; the food is "consistently good" and the "most complete" wine list also wins praise, but what's really "spectacular" is the "sunset view", after which "guests usually stand up and applaud."

**Alexis Baking Company** *Bakery* 22 | 11 | 14 | $17
(aka ABC)

**Napa** | 1517 Third St. (bet. Church & School Sts.) | 707-258-1827 | www.alexisbakingcompany.com

"It's love at first bite" at Downtown Napa's cult bakery and cafe, a real "insiders' place" whipping up "scrumptious, nap-inducing", high-priced breakfasts and lunch fare ("especially the huevos rancheros, awesome burgers" and seasonal sandwiches on "exceptional breads"); although you can "kick off a day of wine tasting" with "coffee and something sweet" at this "funky", "no-frills" counter joint, it's best to "grab and go" since the "erratic service" creates something of "a wait."

**All Seasons Bistro** M *Californian* ∇ 21 | 15 | 18 | $37

**Calistoga** | 1400 Lincoln Ave. (Washington St.) | 707-942-9111 | www.allseasonsnapavalley.net

This Calistoga bistro may fly under the radar, but it hawks the "best wine list in town" since you can "buy a bottle in the shop" next door and "drink it with your meal" for a mere $15 corkage fee; the "well-prepared" Californian fare and modest decor are "nothing to write home about", but oenophiles "go back" for the "fantastic" vino "whenever they're in wine country."

**Angèle** *French* 22 | 22 | 22 | $49

**Napa** | 540 Main St. (3rd St.) | 707-252-8115 | www.angelerestaurant.com

"It's impossible not to be relaxed and happy" at this "waterfront" French bistro where you can linger on the "simply angelic" terrace watching the "lazy" Napa River flow by while enjoying "long European"-style meals and a "few fantastic glasses of wine"; the boathouse's "inviting interior" boasts a "fun bar" that's a big "local" Napa "see and be scene" for those who "make, sell or drink" wine; P.S. "occasionally disappointed" diners hope the post-Survey arrival of a new chef will lift up the menu.

**Annalien** S M *Vietnamese* 24 | 20 | 20 | $36

**Napa** | 1142 Main St. (bet. 1st & Pearl Sts.) | 707-224-8319

"Charming owner" Annalien "greets you personally" at her "gem tucked away in Downtown Napa" serving "colonial-era Vietnamese fare" and "terrific wines by the glass" in a 1930s period setting; forget "bargain $4 pho here - this is upscale stuff", and it's so "exceptional" surveyors say you want to "keep it to yourself"; still, the word is out about this "welcome addition to the challenged ethnic scene" - it's "quickly become popular with locals", so you better be sure to "get there early."

**Applewood Inn & Restaurant** S M *Californian* 24 | 21 | 21 | $49

**Guerneville** | 13555 Hwy. 116 (River Rd.) | 707-869-9093 | www.applewoodinn.com

A "lovely" Guerneville "sleeper" "hidden in the woods" of the Russian River valley, this bed-and-breakfast eatery "beats its ritzier competitors" with locally sourced, "ingredient driven" Californian cuisine ("even the cheese tray was a little work of art") and "outstanding" Sonoma wines; the "lodgy" dining room, anchored by two giant stone fireplaces, and the "accommodating staff" add to the "charm"; N.B. the chef left post-Survey.

## RESTAURANTS

| | FOOD | DECOR | SERVICE | COST |
|---|---|---|---|---|

**Auberge du Soleil** *Californian/French* 25 | 28 | 25 | $81

**Rutherford** | Auberge du Soleil | 180 Rutherford Hill Rd. (Silverado Trail) | 707-967-3111 | www.aubergedusoleil.com

"High above the Silverado Trail", this "first-class", "romantic" Rutherford resort's restaurant beckons travelers with the "whole trifecta" - "sweeping" "vineyard views", "top-notch" Cal-French menus and a "spectacular" wine list navigated by "gently stroking service"; it's a "total sensual immersion" and far "easier to snag reservations than at some of its snootier competition" in Napa Valley; even the cash-strapped admit it's "unbeatable" for breakfast, a "magical" lunch or "cocktails at sunset with some appetizers" on the "glorious deck."

**Azzurro Pizzeria & Enoteca** *Pizza* 23 | 17 | 18 | $23

**Napa** | 1260 Main St. (bet. Clinton & Pearl Sts.) | 707-255-5552

Locals "pass up the expensive wine country eateries" and nosh on pie instead at (ex Tra Vigne) chef Michael Getvan's "laid-back", mid-priced Italian that recently relocated to Downtown Napa; the "in spot" bakes up the "same great", "inventive" thin-crust combos ("who knew cauliflower pizza could be so delish?"), along with "new appetizers", "awesome soft-serve ice cream" and domestic vinos, all in a "hip", larger venue than the original; P.S. be warned: it still "fills up quickly" and gets "super noisy."

NEW **BarBersQ** *BBQ* 22 | 17 | 19 | $32

**Napa** | Bel Aire Plaza | 3900 Bel Aire Plaza (Redwood Rd.) | 707-224-6600 | www.barbersq.com

"Gourmet BBQ might sound like an oxymoron", but the "creative", "Southern-tinged" American menu - upgraded with "free-range meat, organic produce" and a "sophisticated wine list" - at this "informal" Napa "strip-mall" newcomer is winning over "locals" with its "awesome pulled pork" and other affordable "kick-ass" 'cue; despite an "awkward", "loud" room, it's "kid-friendly" and there's a "good vibe."

**Barndiva** M *American* 18 | 22 | 16 | $44

**Healdsburg** | 231 Center St. (Matheson St.) | 707-431-0100 | www.barndiva.com

It's "über-mod minimalism meets home on the range" ("free range", that is) at this Healdsburg hot spot that brings together "avant-garde", "farm-fresh" Traditional American eats and "magnificent cocktails"; locals may squawk over the "minuscule portions" and a staff that takes itself "waaay too seriously", but an "urbane", younger set that's more interested in "socializing" "than in fine dining" digs the "noir-ish" bar scene; P.S. "sitting on the rustic" garden patio "with a blood-orange margarita" is a "slice of heaven."

**Betty's Fish & Chips** 🄼 *Seafood* ▽ 20 | 9 | 16 | $17

**Santa Rosa** | 4046 Sonoma Hwy. (Streamside Dr.) | 707-539-0899

"Why wait until Lent when the fish is this good?" joke Santa Rosa locals who satisfy "hankerings" for "hearty old-fashioned fish 'n' chips" washed down with a "good selection of beer" at this hang on Highway 12; the less-chipper who carped that it was a "hole-in-the-wall" might be pleasantly surprised by a recent nautical-themed makeover.

**Bistro des Copains** *French* 26 | 18 | 22 | $42

**Occidental** | 3782 Bohemian Hwy. (bet. Coleman Valley & Graton Rds.) | 707-874-2436 | www.bistrodescopains.com

"Set your GPS to Occidental" because this "jewel in the woods" is worth finding "among the Italian binge-fests" in the area; "tenderly prepared", locally sourced Provençal bistro classics, a "wine list with some real finds" and an owner who "chats up regulars" give this "river casual" spot its "*gemütlichkeit*"; highlights include "$1 oyster Wednesdays", "no corkage fees on Sonoma wines on Tuesdays" and the "three-course nightly special" (a "steal" on any night).

**Bistro Don Giovanni** *Italian* 23 | 22 | 20 | $46

**Napa** | 4110 Howard Ln. (bet. Oak Knoll & Salvador Aves.) | 707-224-3300 | www.bistrodongiovanni.com

Even "the staff seems to be having fun" at Napa's "iconic", "bustling" Italian trattoria, a "sentimental favorite" packed with "locals, out-of-towners" and a "who's who on the wine scene"; it offers "terrific" Cal-Ital fare, "fabulous vino" and a "dreamy setting among the grapes", but the sprawling dining room gets "raucous"and service can be "sporadtic", so hit it "on the right night" when you can "sit on the outside patio."

🅉 **Bistro Jeanty** *French* 26 | 20 | 22 | $51

**Yountville** | 6510 Washington St. (Mulberry St.) | 707-944-0103 | www.bistrojeanty.com

Francophiles ask "why spend obscene amounts of cash for fancy over-worked dishes elsewhere" when you can "get your pig on" at Philippe

Jeanty's "heart-warming", "French-to-the-core" flagship budget bistro whose "beyond fabulous", "homestyle" country fare proves that "good food doesn't have to be posh nosh"; the "homey digs" (including "outdoor seating" and a "communal table") are "more neighborly", and the service more "friendly", than at some of its "pretentious Yountville neighbors" so "last-minute" diners resoundingly approve.

**Bistro Ralph** ⊠ *Californian/French* 22 | 17 | 22 | $45

**Healdsburg** | 109 Plaza St. (Healdsburg Ave.) | 707-433-1380

"Healdsburg has fancier" spots "but this is *real* Healdsburg" laud loyalists of this "bustling" "fixture" on the Plaza where "Ralphie boy" and his "enthusiastic" crew "keep the locals happy" dishing up "fabulous" Cal-French bistro "standards" "without pretense" and take "rightful pride in Sonoma county wines" (but don't overlook the "outstanding martini menu"); even the "underwhelmed" concede that lunch "outside" is a "fun way to spend the afternoon."

**Boon Fly Café** *Californian* 21 | 19 | 19 | $31

**Napa** | Carneros Inn | 4048 Sonoma Hwy. (Los Carneros Ave.) | 707-299-4900 | www.thecarnerosinn.com

It's "well worth pulling off the Carneros Highway" to this "roadside" Napa "dining adventure", an all-day "cute" "urban"-chic farmhouse cafe in the Carneros Inn plying "fresh doughnuts" at brunch as well as "casual" Californian lunch and dinners that "soak up the alcohol" from wine touring; the "moderately priced" meals and locally leaning vino (priced just over retail) are a "welcome change" from the area's other hot spots, even if it is marred by "variable service."

**Boonville Hotel** *Californian* ∇ 22 | 17 | 19 | $49

**Boonville** | Boonville Hotel | 14050 Hwy. 128 (Lambert Ln.) | 707-895-2210 | www.boonvillehotel.com

"The apple doesn't fall far from the tree" josh fans of this "funky" Boonville roadhouse "run by the son of the founders" of the nearby Apple Farm that serves "satisfying", "simple" seasonal Californian cuisine and Anderson Valley vintages; the "relaxed atmosphere" in the "rustic" Shaker-style dining room makes it "a local favorite", but daydreaming day-trippers "long to be back" "on a lovely summer day" because "nothing's more enjoyable than dinner in the garden."

**Bouchon** ◐ *French* 26 | 23 | 23 | $55

**Yountville** | 6534 Washington St. (Yount St.) | 707-944-8037 | www.frenchlaundry.com

While it's not quite a "junior French Laundry", this brassy French "bistro on steroids" from "Keller Inc.", with its "impeccable", "high-class" "chalkboard menu", "fab" *fruits de mer* and "demi carafes of wine" served "sans the attitude" is about as close to Paris as you can get in "Y'ville"; it's "packed to the gills" all day and "into the night" with locals and tourists who also go "crazy" for the "luscious baked goods" and "foie gras dog biscuits" at the adjacent bakery.

**Bounty Hunter** *BBQ* 17 | 17 | 18 | $33

**Napa** | 975 First St. (Main St.) | 707-226-3976 | www.bountyhunterwine.com

Located near the Napa River, this "neat" Wild West wine bar/retail shop is "entertaining" "before a show at the Opera House" or after "recovering from a day of tastings"; though primarily an oenophile's outlet - the "large assortment" of 400 vins and over 40 "by the glass" is "fun to play in" - the servers "really know" their stuff and the "microscopic kitchen" delivers "the best beer-can chicken" and "satisfying" BBQ ribs from a new smoker.

**Bovolo** *Italian* 22 | 11 | 14 | $25

**Healdsburg** | Copperfield's Bookstore | 106 Matheson St. (Healdsburg Ave.) | 707-431-2962 | www.bovolorestaurant.com

"Best Slow Food in Healdsburg if you want a quick bite" divulge "guinea pigs" ("emphasis on the 'pig' part") who go hog wild, spending "big money" for "small" though "terrific pizzas, sandwiches and gelato" scoops at this zazu offshoot, an Italian cafe and Bellini bar in Copperfield's Bookstore; still, most eschew the "grade-school-cafeteria" interior, prefering to gobble "artisanal salumi" on the "nice" pooch-and-kid-friendly patio; N.B. open for dinner Friday–Sunday (plus Monday and Tuesday June–September), and it has bi-monthly family-style 'Big Night Out' prix fixe menus.

**Brannan's Grill** *American/French* ▽ 20 | 19 | 20 | $43

**Calistoga** | 1374 Lincoln Ave. (Washington St.) | 707-942-2233 | www.brannansgrill.com

"After a long day of wine tasting, a martini and well-prepared steak sound nice" agree admirers who also indulge in "solid" French-

American wine country "comfort food" at this "consistent Calistoga favorite" with a "lively", "historic vibe"; whether you snag a table by the accordion windows for "great people-watching" or chow down at the "fabulous old bar" you're in for a "memorable" meal, especially when the live jazz kicks in on weekends.

**Cafe Beaujolais** *Californian/French* 25 | 21 | 23 | $52

**Mendocino** | 961 Ukiah St. (School St.) | 707-937-5614 | www.cafebeaujolais.com

Bay Area "foodies with unlimited mileage" and North Coast tourists find a "classic" in "Cafe Beauj-alicious" - "a charming little restaurant in an out-of-the-way" Mendocino village presenting "inventive" Cal-French fare and "local wines" in a "romantic" Victorian cottage; although it's "different than it was 10 years ago" due to "changing owners", the "granny's parlor" decor, "gracious servers" and "consistent quality" (plus the reinstatement of lunch) make it "still worth the drive."

**Cafe Citti** *Italian* ▽ 22 | 12 | 16 | $25

**Kenwood** | 9049 Sonoma Hwy./Hwy. 12 (Shaw Ave.) | 707-833-2690

"Sonoma locals" hail the "great Caesar" and other "garlicky" Tuscan goodies like the "simple but flavorful" pasta and roast chicken at this "roadside spot" in Kenwood that's "noisy and cramped" but "fun" and "friendly" like a "trattoria should be"; if Citti-slickers scoff at the "casual wine country counter service" and an "uninspiring" vino list, admirers retort that the "value" prices make it "good for a quickie" between "winery hopping", particularly if you "bring your own" bottle.

**Z Cafe La Haye** S M *American/Californian* 26 | 17 | 23 | $49

**Sonoma** | 140 E. Napa St. (bet. E. 1st & E. 2nd Sts.) | 707-935-5994 | www.cafelahaye.com

While it's "hidden off the Sonoma Plaza", thus "not overrun with tourists", you'll still need rezzies (or get there early) for this "country jewel box" of a restaurant, lest you "miss out on "one of the best" "between San Francisco and Seattle"; the "outstanding" Cal-New American fare produced in a "thumbnail-size kitchen" is "perfectly prepared" by new chef Norman Owens, and complemented by an "exciting" boutique wine list and an "attentive" crew that "never lags."

| | FOOD | DECOR | SERVICE | COST |
|---|---|---|---|---|
| **Carneros Bistro & Wine Bar** *Californian* | ▽ 20 | 20 | 20 | $44 |

**Sonoma** | The Lodge at Sonoma | 1325 Broadway (bet. Clay St. & Leveroni Rd.) | 707-931-2042 | www.thelodgeatsonoma.com

"Not your typical hotel restaurant", this "gorgeously located" "unexpected pleasure" "off the Sonoma Plaza" has a chef who "grows her own herbs in the garden out front" and uses them in Californian "wine country comfort food that does the trick" delivered "with no attitude"; the patio is perfect for savoring a hearty 'Vintner's Breakfast', and oenophiles craving more "after a day of tasting" can dip into the restaurant's all-Carneros cellar.

**Celadon** *American/Eclectic* — 24 | 22 | 23 | $50

**Napa** | The Historic Napa Mill | 500 Main St. (5th St.) | 707-254-9690 | www.celadonnapa.com

Greg Cole's casual Napa Mill outpost may be "surrounded by some of the most impressive restaurants in the world" but locals insist that "dollar for dollar you won't find better" than this Eclectic-New American "go-to" place for an "upscale lunch", a "special night" "by the fireplace on the patio" or when you "just don't want to gamble on a good meal"; as "soothing" as its "celery walls", the riverfront "gem" boasts a "cheerful" crew and "adventurous" global comfort food that "pairs perfectly with the region's wines."

**Central Market** *Californian/Mediterranean* — 23 | 17 | 19 | $40

**Petaluma** | 42 Petaluma Blvd. N. (Western Ave.) | 707-778-9900 | www.centralmarketpetaluma.com

It's "worth the detour off the 101" to this "hip" Petaluma haunt where the Cal-Med menu's "slow roasted" meats (think "carnitas gone to heaven") and "wood-fired pizzas" are "pure Marin"; "exposed brick and high ceilings" set the stage for a "warm and friendly" scene fueled by "well-priced wines" and a "wonderful" chef-owner "who personally greets" each guest and "provides drama in the open kitchen."

**Chapter and Moon** Ⓜ *American* — ▽ 20 | 15 | 21 | $32

**Fort Bragg** | 32150 N. Harbor Dr. (Shoreline Hwy.) | 707-962-1643

"You feel like you're sitting at the edge of the harbor eating right along with the seals" boast Fort Braggers who frequent this low-key fish shack "anytime of day" to "watch the boats come in" while enjoying fin fare so fresh "it's as if you caught it right off the wharf", "gigantic salads" and other American "comfort foods"; the "owners are welcoming", and best of all, it's that rare "affordable" North Coast spot that won't send you into Chapter 11.

**Charcuterie** *French* 23 | 16 | 20 | $35

**Healdsburg** | Healdsburg Plaza | 335 Healdsburg Ave. (Plaza St.) | 707-431-7213

"It's no longer piggy pink" and most of the porcine "tchotchkes" are gone, but this smartly redecorated "casual" all-day French bistro is still the place in Healdsburg to pork out with "charcuterie that's da bomb", meaty entrees and desserts you can't "deny yourself"; it's "not fine dining", but "hits the mark more often than some of the highfalutin" alternatives and boasts an impressive Sonoma-heavy wine list, leaving surveyors crying '*oui oui oui*' all the way home.

**Cindy's Backstreet Kitchen** *American/Californian* 24 | 20 | 22 | $42

**St. Helena** | 1327 Railroad Ave. (bet. Adams St. & Hunt Ave.) | 707-963-1200 | www.cindysbackstreetkitchen.com

"Cindy [Pawlcyn] does it again" at her "upbeat" St. Helena "Mustards offshoot" whose "friendly" vibe and "cozy" "country" kitchen decor make for "a real neighborhood place", even though "you might sit next to a winemaker or celebrity" equally "smitten" by the multiculti Cal-New Americana "home cooking" that "flirts with greatness"; its alfresco lunch "under the fig tree" is also "popular among tourists" because, given the local "alternatives", prices here won't put you "out on the street."

**Cole's Chop House** *Steak* 24 | 22 | 23 | $65

**Napa** | 1122 Main St. (bet. 1st & Pearl Sts.) | 707-224-6328 | www.coleschophouse.com

"Carnivorous" types cap their "winery touring" by "getting their fix" at this "wonderful", "classy", "very masculine" "meat-lover's mecca and cardiologist's nightmare" in a historic stone building overlooking Napa Creek; Celadon owner "Greg Cole spares no $$$" for his "quality" "aged steaks" and neither will you, but with "those incredible" hash brown potatoes, "giant" "martooneys" and "as you'd expect, fantastic" regional reds, the only question is "who's driving?"

| Restaurant | FOOD | DECOR | SERVICE | COST |
|---|---|---|---|---|
| **Cook St. Helena** *Italian* | 24 | 14 | 22 | $39 |

**St. Helena** | 1310 Main St. (Hunt Ave.) | 707-963-7088
"Vintners" are among the "Napa Valley elite" who "squeeze in with the locals" at St. Helena's "under-the-radar" "hole-in-the-wall" that "keeps them coming back" for "fantastic", "unpretentious" moderately priced fare that conjures fantasies of "the wonderful Northern Italian grandmother you never had"; the "cozy" and "welcoming" if "almost chaotic atmosphere" befits a "casual lunch" in a day of "wine tasting"; N.B. closes at 5 PM Sundays.

| Restaurant | FOOD | DECOR | SERVICE | COST |
|---|---|---|---|---|
| **Cucina Paradiso** *Italian* | 24 | 14 | 22 | $34 |

**Petaluma** | Golden Eagle Shopping Ctr. | 56 E. Washington St. (Petaluma Blvd.) | 707-782-1130 | www.cucinaparadisopetaluma.com
"Heavenly" fare awaits inside this "benign-looking" "neighborhood spot" "tucked away" in a "run-down strip mall" testify disciples of the Southern Italian "favorite" "just steps from the Petaluma riverfront"; the "dream-worthy homemade pasta" and "fabulous meat and fish dishes" are "better than you'll find at swank restaurants for triple the price"; the "only drawback" is a "cozy at best" interior, which is prone to promoting "very long waits", luckily "service is much better than" the setting.

| Restaurant | FOOD | DECOR | SERVICE | COST |
|---|---|---|---|---|
| **Cuvée** *American* | 20 | 22 | 18 | $43 |

**Napa** | 1650 Soscol Ave. (Vallejo St.) | 707-224-2330 | www.cuveenapa.com
Catering to both Napa "locals and tourists", this "off-the-beaten-track" replacement for the late "great Budo" on the edge of the up-and-coming Oxbow District offers American comfort food and an extensive wine list; the setting includes a "nice outdoor dining area" for lunch and a "lively bar" specializing in local wines on tap that's the "cool" "place to be during happy hour"; but "service that can be so-so" keeps surveyors from bubbling over with enthusiasm.

| Restaurant | FOOD | DECOR | SERVICE | COST |
|---|---|---|---|---|
| **Z Cyrus** *French* | 29 | 27 | 28 | $117 |

**Healdsburg** | Les Mars Hotel | 29 North St. (Healdsburg Ave.) | 707-433-3311 | www.cyrusrestaurant.com
Douglas Keane's "haute" New French "tour de force" with global influences is a "brilliant" "reason to go to" Healdsburg say those enraptured by his "almost flawless" "masterpieces" that include "opulent" and

"stunning" "design-it-yourself" prix fixe and tasting menus that are "fit for royalty" and priced accordingly; "from the caviar and champagne cart" to "foie gras three ways" delivered by "pampering" "synchronized servers" beneath grand vaulted ceilings, it's all "pure theatrics" and "off the charts"; N.B. à la carte at the bar only.

**Della Fattoria Downtown Café** Ⓜ *Bakery/Eclectic* 25 | 16 | 19 | $25

**Petaluma** | 141 Petaluma Blvd. N. (bet. Washington St. & Western Ave.) | 707-763-0161 | www.dellafattoria.com

When they "can't manage to grab a loaf" of this bakery's "fabulous bread" at the farmer's market, carbophiles "drive up to Petaluma" to "indulge" in the manna directly from the source, where owners "as warm as their baked goods" run a "folksy", "fine" and affordable Eclectic "little cafe" serving "rustic" breakfasts, "pristine salads", "incredible desserts" and "big bowls of cafe latte"; just "get there early" as it only stays open for dinner on Fridays.

**Della Santina's** *Italian* 20 | 17 | 20 | $38

**Sonoma** | 133 E. Napa St. (1st St.) | 707-935-0576 | www.dellasantinas.com

It's "like eating in an Italian garden" enthuse "food-loving Sonomans" who linger "under the grapevines on the patio" at this "deservedly popular" "family-owned" corner trattoria just off the Plaza known for "authentic", midpriced "Lucca-style" *cucina* – especially the "heavenly gnocchi" and "meats cooked on the rotisserie"; a fireplace and a "friendly owner" add warmth to the "tiny" interior, and the "outstanding" new adjacent enoteca offers more elbow room for sampling an international list of "good wines."

**Deuce** Ⓜ *American* ∇ 22 | 16 | 20 | $39

**Sonoma** | 691 Broadway (Andrieux St.) | 707-933-3823 | www.dine-at-deuce.com

Guests confide it's akin to "going to someone's house for dinner" when they sit down to "dependable" New American fare at this "very pleasant" "local favorite" with a "lovely garden" off Sonoma Plaza; it's owned by the "nicest couple", plus the "low-key" farmhouse setting "belies a sophisticated kitchen"; add in a "wonderful" wine list that showcases "options from small wineries you won't find" elsewhere and it's easy to see why it's "worth a visit."

| | FOOD | DECOR | SERVICE | COST |
|---|---|---|---|---|

**NEW Diavola Pizzeria & Salumeria** *Italian* | - | - | - | M |

**Geyserville** | 21021 Geyserville Ave. (Highway 128) | 707-814-0111 | www.diavolapizzeria.com

A casual, all-day counterpoint to sibling Santi (also in Geyserville), this rustic, brick-walled pizzeria and salumeria slakes the thirst and hunger of wine country travelers with humble Italian *cucina povera* (peasant food); the midpriced menu features wood-fired, thin-crust pizzas and housemade charcuterie, washed down with Peroni on tap or a slate of L'Italia-only vinos.

**Downtown Bakery & Creamery** ⊭ *Bakery* | 22 | 10 | 15 | $16 |

**Healdsburg** | 308A Center St. (Matheson St.) | 707-431-2719 | www.downtownbakery.net

Wake up and "smell the bread" (and coffee) at this "long-standing" Healdsburg patisserie that bakes up "spectacular pastries", "pants-shrinking" sticky buns and "breakfast pizzas"; the tiny, budget-friendly European-style cafe also serves "alfresco" lunches on the sidewalk or makes them to go, so there's "no need to go anywhere else" "to stoke up after a bike ride" or before a day of wine tasting; N.B. not open for dinner.

**Dry Creek Kitchen** *American* | 24 | 24 | 21 | $64 |

**Healdsburg** | Hotel Healdsburg | 317 Healdsburg Ave. (Matheson St.) | 707-431-0330 | www.charliepalmer.com

Charlie Palmer conveys a "big-city" feel in "sleepy Healdsburg" with his "wonderful" New American "wine-country cuisine" that celebrates all things local in à la carte and "signature" tasting menus served in a "casually elegant" setting to a crowd that's more "glitterati" than "grape-grower"; a wine list that's "a treasure trove of Sonoma" and a "no corkage" policy on BYO regional bottles also help "pack them in"; the generally "well-informed" service can be so "slow"-paced it creaks, still, most find this "fabulous place" "keeps them happy" and "delivers on its celebrity promise."

**Duck Club, The** *American* | 20 | 20 | 21 | $50 |

**Bodega** | Bodega Bay Lodge & Spa | 103 S. Hwy. 1 (Doran Park Rd.) | 707-875-3525 | www.bodegabaylodge.com

"Oversize salon chairs match the large portions" of American eats at this "quiet, serene" quartet that keeps swimming along by providing "solid options" for "leisurely" "well- prepared" Sunday brunches and "festive holiday meals" ("the Easter Bunny even makes a visit"); there's "excellent duck" on the menu (and "pictures of ducks" on the walls); "beautiful" water views enhance the "Monterey and Bodega Bay locations", though elsewhere the "hotel-like" decor makes the feel "totally adrift."

**El Dorado Kitchen** *Californian/Mediterranean* 21 | 22 | 21 | $47

**Sonoma** | El Dorado Hotel | 405 First St. W. (Spain St.) | 707-996-3030 | www.eldoradosonoma.com

On the "Sonoma Plaza scene", this "relaxing" eatery "known as EDK" in the El Dorado Hotel offers "delicious" "upscale" Cal-Med fare "without the pretense" of some other wine country choices; "lapses in service are made up for" by the "beautiful ambiance on the patio under the fig tree" and a "great selection of house drinks" and "splits", causing some to sigh "too bad we couldn't get a room"; N.B. the adjacent Kitchenette serves pastries and sandwiches till 3 PM.

**Étoile** *Californian* 25 | 26 | 25 | $76

**Yountville** | Domaine Chandon Winery | 1 California Dr. (Solano Ave.) | 707-944-2892 | www.chandon.com

Enjoying "lunch on the terrace" after a tour of the Domaine Chandon Winery while sipping bubbly "in the middle of the vineyard" remains the "quintessential Napa Valley experience", while indoors the "beautifully redone" dining room proffers impressive Californian à la carte and tasting menus and wines with "elegant service" in a "classy" setting; the "sophisticated" "experience" comes "without the noise" "of the other Yountville restaurants", except perhaps at the "nightclublike" bar area; N.B. jackets recommended in the evening.

**Farm** *American* 25 | 26 | 22 | $55

**Napa** | Carneros Inn | 4048 Sonoma Hwy. (Old Sonoma Hwy.) | 707-299-4882 | www.thecarnerosinn.com

"Gentleman farmer might be a more appropriate name" for this "spectacular", "stylish" "PlumpJack's outpost" in the Carneros Inn with "views and chews" that are "some of Napa's best in recent vintage"; the New American "artisan cooking at its rural (and local) best" is "too upscale" with "prices a bit high" for the barnyard, but sophisticates can enjoy a "gorgeous alfresco dining experience" or "drinks by the outside fire pit" while taking advantage of "half bottles" of Carneros wines.

## Farmhouse Inn & Restaurant *Californian* — 26 | 24 | 25 | $75

**Forestville** | Farmhouse Inn | 7871 River Rd. (bet. Trenton & Wohler Rds.) | 707-887-3300 | www.farmhouseinn.com

"Driving through vineyards to reach this" "quaint" "restored" farmhouse in the "bucolic woods of Forestville" feels like visiting "a small country inn in France", only here the "amazing" menu and wine list reflect the local Californian terroir through dishes such as rabbit prepared three ways and "a cheese course that rocks"; "served by a staff that's unobtrusive and impeccable"; the "expensive but awesome" experience is "not as flashy" as other "hyped" wine-country "heavyweights", but regulars insist "there's no finer place to celebrate Sonoma life."

## fig cafe & winebar *French* — 23 | 18 | 23 | $35

**Glen Ellen** | 13690 Arnold Dr. (bet. Horn Ave. & Odonnell Ln.) | 707-938-2130 | www.thefigcafe.com

"Locals line up at 5:30 PM to snag a seat" for an evening of "wine country greatness without the corkage fees" at this no-reservations Glen Ellen "hangout" on the "town square" that's a more casual "alternative to the girl & the fig"; "BYOB" "brings 'em in the door" but the "affordable" "lovely French peasant food", "sincere" staff and a wine list that works for diners who've "tired of Chardonnay" "keep them coming back."

## Flavor *Californian/Eclectic* — 20 | 18 | 16 | $28

**Santa Rosa** | 96 Old Courthouse Sq. (bet. 3rd & 4th Sts.) | 707-573-9600 | www.flavorbistro.com

With "flavors that are all over the map, there's something for every taste" at this "totally affordable" all-day Cal-Eclectic Downtown Santa Rosa bistro "right in Old Courtyard Square" that's a neighborhood fall-back for "no stress dinners", weekend breakfast and "after the movies"; it's "pass-the-earplugs" "noisy" with "slow service" but "bang for the buck" "half portions" and an "extensive wine list" make it "a hidden wine-country bargain."

## NEW Folio Enoteca & Winery *Californian/Mediterranean* — ▽ 23 | 21 | 20 | $24

**Napa** | Oxbow Public Mkt. | 610 First St. (McKinstry St.) | 707-256-3700 | www.foliowine.com

At Michael Mondavi's "pleasant", affordable new wine bar in Napa's "bustling" Oxbow Public Market, customers can sip (on Folio's

Oberon, I'M and Hangtime brands) and snack on former Robert Mondavi winery chef Sarah Scott's "fabulous" Cal-Med fare while watching it being prepared, thanks to a glassed-in micro winery and an open kitchen; you can dine at the bar fashioned from reclaimed oak barrels, as well as at tables, from 11 AM–7 PM daily.

**Foothill Grille** Ⓢ Ⓜ *American* ∇ 20 | 13 | 18 | $39

**Napa** | La Quevana | 2766 Old Sonoma Rd. (Foothill Blvd.) | 707-257-2270

Fans rejoice that the Traditional American fare (including "excellent" "wood-roasted" prime rib) is as "delicious as ever" at Jerry Schaffer's "longtime neighborhood favorite" in Napa ever since he "came back to reclaim" the helm; a low corkage fee (waived on Wednesdays) adds to the "good value", but some diners are "disappointed" by the "slimmer, less expensive menu" and staff they describe as "eager, but untrained", lamenting that it's lost some of its "former excellence."

Ⓩ **French Laundry, The** *American/French* 29 | 26 | 28 | $264

**Yountville** | 6640 Washington St. (Creek St.) | 707-944-2380 | www.frenchlaundry.com

"Set your sights high and expect them to be exceeded" at Thomas Keller's "gustatory temple" in Yountville, a "once-in-a-lifetime gastronomic event" ("who can afford it twice?") that reclaims this Survey's No. 1 Food ranking for its "exhilarating" French-New American tasting menus that are "pure pleasure from the first bite to the last"; the "service is a seamless extension of the kitchen", "coddling and cosseting" foodies who've managed to "magically score a table" inside the "country manor house" setting, where the "complete experience" equals "four hours" of sheer "bliss."

**Fumé Bistro & Bar** *American* 21 | 16 | 19 | $40

**Napa** | 4050 Byway E. (Wine Country Ave.) | 707-257-1999 | www.fumebistro.com

"Shhh" whisper Napa "locals", for "the tourists haven't fully discovered" this "reliable" New American bistro that "makes good use of its wood-burning oven" to crank out "great pizzas" and other "nice middle-of-the-road" "comfort food" at "decent prices"; the service is "friendly", and while some say it's "noisy" and find its "proximity to Highway 29" "off- putting", it remains a "favorite" "everyday spot" for many.

**Gary Chu's** M *Chinese* 21 | 18 | 19 | $30

**Santa Rosa** | 611 Fifth St. (bet. D St. & Mendocino Ave.) | 707-526-5840 | www.garychus.com

"Consistently pleasurable", the Chu family's "creative" Chinese spot is "one of the busiest restaurants in Santa Rosa" serving a "small", "up-to-date" menu studded with "favorites" like "delightful" whole fish and "especially well-liked" tea-smoked duck; still, choosier types tut the decor is "outdated" and the fare "unexceptional."

**girl & the fig, the** *French* 23 | 20 | 21 | $42

**Sonoma** | Sonoma Hotel | 110 W. Spain St. (1st St.) | 707-938-3634 | www.thegirlandthefig.com

A "gem" in the "heart of wine country", this Sonoma French offers "truly comforting" "traditional bistro fare", served by a "gracious" staff in a "casual" setting; many praise the "excellent local" *vin* list, although a few are put off by its "focus on Rhônes-style wines"; prepare to get "friendly with other diners" in the "tight" interior, which is why insiders prefer the "lovely" "secret garden" outside.

**Go Fish** *Eclectic/Seafood* 23 | 22 | 20 | $49

**St. Helena** | 641 Main St. (Mills Ln.) | 707-963-0700 | www.gofishrestaurant.net

Cindy Pawlcyn (Cindy's Backstreet Kitchen, Mustards Grill) "deals a winning hand" at her "bright and airy" Eclectic seafooder in St. Helena, a "great catch" in "the valley of red wine and meat", serving "creative", "modern" takes on fin fare, including "melt-in-your-mouth sushi", courtesy of Ken Tominaga (of Rohnert Park's Hana); it's "comfortable" in the "beautiful" space with a large outdoor bar, but while fans insist the service has "improved" of late, others rate it "poor for the prices."

Z **Hana Japanese Restaurant** S M *Japanese* 26 | 15 | 20 | $46

**Rohnert Park** | 101 Golf Course Dr. (Roberts Lake Rd.) | 707-586-0270 | www.hanajapanese.com

"Don't let the location fool you" advise fans, for Ken Tominaga's "surprisingly hip" "strip-mall" Japanese in Rohnert Park serves "perfect cuts" of "sparkling fresh" sushi that some call the best "north of the Golden Gate Bridge", as well as "excellent" cooked fare; "adventurous" sorts with "discriminating palates" sit at the bar, where service is "more attentive" and Ken creates "outrageously delicious" omakase meals "just for you."

| | FOOD | DECOR | SERVICE | COST |
|---|---|---|---|---|

**NEW Healdsburg Bar & Grill** *American* | - | - | - | M |

**Healdsburg** | 245 Healdsburg Ave. (bet. Matheson & Mill Sts.) | 707-433-3333 | www.healdsburgbarandgrill.com

Even under its new owners (the Cyrus team), this long-running casual grill remains a low-key, kid-friendly alternative to Healdsburg's fancier haunts; the Traditional American menu, upgraded with grade-A ingredients but still moderately priced, includes build-your-own burgers and pizzas, and is complemented by craft beers and local vinos - both serious vintages and 'patio wines', which presumably go down best on the spacious, shaded outdoor dining area.

**NEW Hopmonk Tavern** *Eclectic* | - | - | - | M |

**Sebastopol** | 230 Petaluma Ave. (Sebastopol Ave.) | 707-829-7300 | www.hopmonk.com

Smack in the middle of wine country, this hopping tavern set in a historic 105-year-old stone-and-timber building in Downtown Sebastopol showcases international craft beers selected by owner Dean Biersch (co-founder of Gordon Biersch) and his beer sommelier, complemented by an all-day, locally sourced Eclectic gastropub menu; an outdoor beer garden and adjacent live-music venue add to the brew.

**Hurley's Restaurant & Bar** *Californian/Mediterranean* | 17 | 18 | 20 | $42 |

**Yountville** | 6518 Washington St. (Yount St.) | 707-944-2345 | www.hurleysrestaurant.com

This "cute", "casual" downtown Yountville grill is "popular with the locals" who "sit out on the patio sipping wine" over a "bargain" "vintner lunch" or hang at the bar for a late-night snack; given that it's in the "great foodie town" of "Kellerville", the Cal-Med meals - though "especially cozy by the fireplace" is "not particularly exciting."

**In-N-Out Burger** ◐ *Burgers* | 21 | 9 | 17 | $8 |

**Napa** | 820 Imola Ave./Hwy. 121 (Napa Valley Hwy.) | 800-786-1000 | www.in-n-out.com

If "only they would double-double the number of locations" beef boosters of these "legendary" West Coast "'50s-style" fast-food "classics" where a "limited menu" of "freshly made" burgers, "hand-cut fries" and "spoonably thick shakes" - "all for less" than the competition charges - ensures that the "16-year-old behind the counter" will get you "in and out quickly"; to feel like a regular, study the website's "insider's lingo" on the "not-so-secret menu" ("hint: don't ask for vegetable or mineral").

**Jimtown Store** *Deli* 18 | 15 | 15 | $18

**Healdsburg** | 6706 Hwy. 128 (Chaffee Rd.) | 707-433-1212 | www.jimtown.com

"Way off the beaten path" in Healdsburg, this "kitschy" country kitchen and general store looks like a "throwback" to a "bygone era", with "delicious" "high-end" breakfasts and sandwiches you can enjoy with a "good glass of wine" on the "funky" patio or take out for a picnic "among the vineyards"; just "don't stop if you're in a big hurry", as it's "impossible to get in and out without buying an odd trinket or toy."

**John Ash & Co.** *Californian* 23 | 25 | 23 | $57

**Santa Rosa** | 4330 Barnes Rd. (River Rd.) | 707-527-7687 | www.vintnersinn.com

With a "gorgeous setting among the vineyards", "exceptional wine list" and "uniquely prepared" Californian fare "plucked straight from their garden", this "pricey" Santa Rosa "wine country tradition" remains the "gold standard" for "Sonoma county residents and visitors" who come for "special occasions", "outdoor dining on warm summer evenings" and "after-work drinks" in the "remodeled bar" ("Martini Mondays . . . doesn't get better than that!"); P.S. after 20 years, chef Jeffrey Madura – who took over from namesake "TV personality" Ash – left post-Survey.

NEW **JoLe** M *American* - | - | - | M

**Calistoga** | Mount View Hotel | 1457 Lincoln Ave. (Washington St.) | 707-942-5938 | www.jolerestaurant.com

This *très jolie* Calistoga arrival, located in the Mount View Hotel, features midpriced farm-to-table New American cuisine from the husband-and-wife team who previously owned Philadelphia's Matyson; a tiled brick oven doubles as the focal point of the dining room and six-seat chef's counter, while microbrews and boutique old-world wines are poured at the newly constructed wooden bar.

**Julia's Kitchen** *Californian/French* 23 | 20 | 22 | $52

**Napa** | COPIA | 500 First St. (bet. Silverado Trail & Soscol Ave.) | 707-265-5700 | www.juliaskitchen.org

Napa visitors "make a detour" to this "tribute" to the "Patron Saint of American food" for its "bounty" of Cal-French fare featuring "treats from the on-site gardens" and the "freshest meats and fish"; however, despite a recent paint job, a few feel the "corporate" setting inside the COPIA food museum is too "sterile" and the "froufrou" dinner menu (plus Friday and Saturday lunch) "lacks the heart and humanity" of the "indomitable Ms. Child"; N.B. an adjacent wine bar was slated to open at press time.

**K&L Bistro** ☒ *French* 24 | 16 | 20 | $45

**Sebastopol** | 119 S. Main St. (Bodega Ave.) | 707-823-6614

"Stroll into mini-Paris" at this "lovely", "friendly" little French bistro in downtown Sebastopol that sates cravings for "authentic" Gallic fare with "substantial portions" of "high-quality food" and a "fine wine list"; though tables are "tightly packed", most say it's "well worth the trip."

**Kenwood** Ⓜ *American/French* ∇ 23 | 20 | 23 | $50

**Kenwood** | 9900 Sonoma Hwy./Hwy. 12 (Warm Springs Rd.) | 707-833-6326 | www.kenwoodrestaurant.com

Nothing "epitomizes" "casual wine country dining" like this "bright, cheerful" "oldie but goodie" roadhouse in Kenwood; the "midpriced" New American-French fare and "terrific wine" offerings "rarely change", but they're "always outstanding" and "served all day" by a "cheerful" crew; sure, the digs are "charming" and the "chatty bar" alluring, but loyalists insist that "nothing's better" than a meal on the "beautiful patio" overlooking the vineyards.

**LaSalette** *Portuguese* 22 | 18 | 22 | $42

**Sonoma** | Mercado Ctr. | 452 First St. E., Suite H (bet. Napa & Spain Sts.) | 707-938-1927 | www.lasalette-restaurant.com

"What food!" marvel fans of this "adorable" "tucked-away gem off the Sonoma Plaza" purveying "Portuguese down-home cuisine" that includes "terrific" specialties and "outstanding breads" from its wood-burning oven; there's "not much to see" on the decor front, but the vibe is "lively" thanks to the "husband-and-wife owners" who make "even strangers feel welcome"; its Portugal-heavy wine list helps make this a "nice change of pace from the other (more touristy) places around."

**La Toque** Ⓜ *French* 26 | - | 25 | $127

**Napa** | Westin Verasa | 1314 McKinstry St. (Soscol Ave.) | 707-257-5157 | www.latoque.com

Ken Frank's "special-occasion" wine country respite is like a "Mercedes-Benz: professional, reliable and luxurious", with "top-of-the-line" service featuring "world-class" sommelier Scott Tracy, who personally pairs "wonderful boutique and unusual wines" with the "flawless" French tasting menus (including annual truffle fetes); a planned September '08 move from Rutherford to "larger" Downtown digs at Napa's Westin Verasa (1314 McKinstry Street) should please patrons who found that its old space to be a "downer", and its expanded menu with less-expensive prix fixes may sate savers who've nicknamed it "La Broke."

**Ledford House** Ⓜ *Californian/Mediterranean* ∇ 24 | 22 | 23 | $48

**Albion** | 3000 N. Hwy. 1 (Spring Grove Rd.) | 707-937-0282 | www.ledfordhouse.com

"Spectacular ocean" vistas, a "welcoming atmosphere", "attentive owners" "directly involved in preparing" the "ultrafresh", "hearty unpretentious" Cal-Med fare and "solid wine choices" make this "unbeatable location" on a bluff in the Albion headlands a "definite must for a fogless sunset dinner on the Mendocino coast"; music aficionados suggest "skip dinner" (served Wednesday-Sunday only) and head to the bar for nightly jazz and the same "view that won't quit."

**Little River Inn** *Californian/Seafood* 22 | 21 | 23 | $42

**Little River** | Little River Inn | 7901 N. Hwy. 1 (Little River Airport Rd.) | 707-937-5942 | www.littleriverinn.com

"Gabby, friendly bartenders" and a "welcoming" staff "tempt you to stay forever" at this "charming" Cal seafooder on the Mendocino coast with "lovely garden views through the huge windows"; whether you order "delicious entrees" in the main dining room, "fantastic fish 'n' chips at the bar" or the "memorable" Swedish hotcakes at the "great Sunday brunch", you'll be "impressed" by this Little River choice; nitpickers, however, note that the fare "has the potential to be a little better."

**MacCallum House** *Californian* 23 | 22 | 20 | $48

**Mendocino** | MacCallum House Inn | 45020 Albion St. (bet. Hesser & Kasten Sts.) | 707-937-5763 | www.maccallumhouse.com

The "charming ambiance" of this "quaint" restaurant/inn occupying a "historic" Mendocino Victorian makes "you feel like you've stepped back in time" but the seasonal, organic Californian cuisine is thoroughly "modern"; "tourists" flock to "breakfast on the deck" while locals prefer the less "spendy" "casual fare" in the Gray Whale Bar with its "roaring fire, slouchy couches" and "great ocean views."

**Madrona Manor** Ⓜ *American/French* | 26 | 26 | 25 | $74

**Healdsburg** | Madrona Manor | 1001 Westside Rd. (W. Dry Creek Rd.) | 707-433-4231 | www.madronamanor.com

When it's time to "celebrate a special occasion", Healdsburgers head to the "cozy confines" of this converted Victorian mansion, an "inn-credible" inn and "world-class" American-French restaurant; the experience is "extraordinary from top to bottom": "superb food"; nearly perfect service and a "quiet, romantic setting" (the veranda is worthy of "a Jane Austen novel"); P.S. for the ultimate experience, the "tasting menu with wine pairings is the way to go."

**Manzanita** Ⓢ Ⓜ *Californian/Mediterranean* | 20 | 18 | 19 | $43

**Healdsburg** | 336 Healdsburg Ave. (North St.) | 707-433-8111 | www.manzanita336.com

"Hearty", "unpretentious" Cal-Med cuisine, including "fantastic" pizzas from the "manzanita wood-burning oven" and a "lovely tasting menu" on Thursdays, along with "friendly" service and a "comfortable" setting make this a "solid" Healdsburg spot "without the fuss of the big-name places"; P.S. there's "no corkage fee on local wines" (max two bottles), so it's a cheaper and "great way to finish off a day" touring wineries.

**Market** *American* | 22 | 20 | 21 | $40

**St. Helena** | 1347 Main St. (bet. Adams St. & Hunt Ave.) | 707-963-3799 | www.marketsthelena.com

When they "want a break from froufrou food", St. Helena habitués head for this "dependable" "down-home" hang with "haute" Traditional American "comfort food" like the "to-die-for" mac 'n' cheese with "a slight twist"; it's "warm, welcoming" and "reasonably priced"; N.B. under new ownership.

**Z Martini House** *American* | 26 | 25 | 24 | $63

**St. Helena** | 1245 Spring St. (bet. Main St. & Oak Ave.) | 707-963-2233 | www.martinihouse.com

"The garden is beautiful when it's warm, the fireplaces cozy when it's not" at this "beautiful, lodgelike" Pat Kuleto-designed "gem" in a converted St. Helena Craftsman home; chef Todd Humphries is a fungus fanatic, so expect "sophisticated mushroom dishes" on the "superb" New American menu, all with a "hefty price tag"; but even for just a bite in the "must-see" "cellar bar", it's "an experience to remember."

| | FOOD | DECOR | SERVICE | COST |
|---|---|---|---|---|
| **Meadowood, The Grill** *Californian* | ▽ 20 | 21 | 22 | $51 |

**St. Helena** | Meadowood Napa Valley | 900 Meadowood Ln. (Silverado Trail) | 707-963-3646 | www.meadowood.com

"No wonder" President "Bush chose to stay" at the Meadowood in St. Helena – with its "lovely surroundings" and "resort atmosphere", it feels like a "hidden gem in Napa Valley"; an alternative to their high-end restaurant, the "casual" Californian grill on-site boasts a "top-notch" setting "overlooking the golf course" and a "beautiful" terrace just made for an "unrushed" breakfast or lunch; stop by for a "relaxing" dinner "after wine tasting all day" and "you won't want to leave."

| | FOOD | DECOR | SERVICE | COST |
|---|---|---|---|---|
| **Z Meadowood, The Restaurant** [S] *Californian* | 26 | 26 | 26 | $89 |

**St. Helena** | Meadowood Napa Valley | 900 Meadowood Ln. (Silverado Trail) | 707-967-1205 | www.meadowood.com

"Meadowood finally has a world-class restaurant" cheer fans who are "blown away" by this "retooled Napa Valley wunderkind" with "divine" prix fixe Californian menus and "elegant service", all "nestled in the woods" at a St. Helena resort; despite a recent chef change, "early indications are very promising" under new toque Christopher Kostow (ex Chez TJ); P.S. those interested in over-indulging in the "perfect wine pairings" may want to book a room at the resort.

| | FOOD | DECOR | SERVICE | COST |
|---|---|---|---|---|
| **Mendo Bistro** *American* | ▽ 24 | 15 | 20 | $38 |

**Fort Bragg** | The Company Store | 301 N. Main St., 2nd fl. (Redwood St.) | 707-964-4974 | www.mendobistro.com

Chef "Nicholas Petti has just gotten better and better" boast Fort Braggers, who claim you "can't go wrong with anything" on the "creative" New American menu, particularly the "fabulous crab cakes"; a "comfortable setting on Main Street" and "reasonable prices" also lead loyalists to say "this is our restaurant of choice when we are dressed up for special occasions or dressed down for an after-work dinner."

| | FOOD | DECOR | SERVICE | COST |
|---|---|---|---|---|
| **Mendocino Hotel** *Californian* | ▽ 18 | 21 | 19 | $35 |

**Mendocino** | Mendocino Hotel | 45080 Main St. (Kasten St.) | 707-937-0511 | www.mendocinohotel.com

There's "new zest" in the Californian menu agree admirers who find it a "joy to sit" in the Mendocino Hotel's supposedly haunted Victorian dining room with "dark" but "charming period decor" or the more casual garden room and nosh on "traditional and unusual dishes"; "check out" the "beautiful wood bar" in the lobby and sip a drink under the "stained-glass dome" - it's quite the "local gathering spot"; still, ghostbusters sigh this "location deserves better."

### Meritage Martini Oyster Bar & Grille *Italian*

▽ 20 | 18 | 18 | $40

**Sonoma** | 165 W. Napa St. (bet. 1st & 2nd Sts.) | 707-938-9430 | www.sonomameritage.com

The chef-owner "works hard to make sure you're happy", whether you fancy a "great variety" of "seafood platters", Northern Italian options like "good osso buco" or even a five-course vegetarian tasting menu; the "unusual combination" of choices, "excellent wine list" and expansive space strike the "right chord" with Sonomans, who "keep going back."

### Mirepoix ⊠S ⊠M *French*

25 | 17 | 24 | $48

**Windsor** | 275 Windsor River Rd. (Honsa Ave.) | 707-838-0162 | www.restaurantmirepoix.com

A "husband-and-wife team" bring "a lovely little bit of France" to Windsor at this "tiny" bistro that's "about as unpretentious as you can get"; the "excellent" "seasonal menu never disappoints", nor does the "innovative wine selection", which is largely from local "boutique producers"; in sum, it's "quite a value" in a "cozy" and "romantic setting."

### Model Bakery *Bakery*

20 | 10 | 13 | $13

**Napa** | Oxbow Public Mkt. | 610 First St. (McKinstry St.) | 707-963-8192
**St. Helena** | 1357 Main St. (bet. Adams St. & Hunt Ave.) | 707-963-8192
www.themodelbakery.com

"Perfect for breakfast" - try the "rich pastries" with a side of "local gossip" - and a "good stopover for a sandwich" on "amazing fresh-baked bread" or a "sweet snack", this art deco bakery in "beautiful St. Helena" (with a Napa sib) "feels like France"; still, a few loafers who meet their "buddies for coffee" caution that surrounding diners may "eavesdrop", and lament that the "Gen Next" servers are in another "cosmos."

### Monti's Rotisserie & Bar *American/Mediterranean*

20 | 19 | 18 | $36

**Santa Rosa** | Montgomery Village Shopping Ctr. | 714 Village Ct. (Farmers Ln.) | 707-568-4404 | www.montisroti.net

"Forget about the shopping-center location" - this "lively" (some say "loud") New American-Med small-plates specialist with a "wonderfully diverse" menu is a "wise choice" in Santa Rosa; the "wood-fired oven" does double duty, cooking the "rotisserie meats and fowl" and upping the "warm and cozy" factor on "dreary winter days"; it may "not quite be up to" owner Mark Stark's other eateries (Willi's Wine Bar and Seafood), but it's still "solid."

**Moosse Café** *Californian* ▽ 23 | 19 | 20 | $39

**Mendocino** | The Blue Heron Inn | 390 Kasten St. (Albion St.) | 707-937-4323 | www.themoosse.com

You can keep "warm by the fire in the winter" and sit out in the "amazing garden in summer" at this "informal" "little place" in the Blue Heron Inn; "excellent", "inventive" Californian cuisine, including "great nightly fish specials", is prepared by one of Mendocino's "reigning chefs", making it a "find" and a "return-to place"; N.B. on Mondays, there's a three-course $20 dinner; N.B. closed Tuesday-Wednesday in winter.

**Mosaic Restaurant & Wine Lounge** *Californian* ▽ 26 | 22 | 23 | $50

**Forestville** | 6675 Front St. (off Mirabel Rd.) | 707-887-7503 | www.mosaiceats.com

"What a find!" exclaim adventurers, who liken this "up-and-coming gem" "in the tiny town of Forestville" to "a prized truffle in the woods" because the chef-owner turns out "exquisite, elegant" Californian cuisine; though "nondescript on the outside", it's "lovely and welcoming" within, with "attentive" servers and a "very cozy atmosphere"; P.S. "if weather permits, dine on the back patio under the beautiful Sonoma skies."

**Mustards Grill** *American/Californian* 24 | 19 | 22 | $47

**Yountville** | 7399 St. Helena Hwy./Hwy. 29 (bet. Oakville Grade Rd. & Washington St.) | 707-944-2424 | www.mustardsgrill.com

Chef/co-owner Cindy Pawlcyn's "exhilarating" "standby" in Yountville – the "original" restaurant in her mini-"foodie empire" – is "everything a great roadhouse is supposed to be", serving "home-cooked food" in a "friendly" if sometimes "frenetic" setting; "regardless of what you order", "you can't go wrong" with the "hearty" Cal-New American cuisine "made with fresh local ingredients", especially if "you don't want to spend a fortune"; maybe that's why it's a "longtime favorite" of locals, who call it "Napa's neighborhood kitchen."

**Napa General Store** *Californian/Eclectic* 19 17 17 $27

**Napa** | 540 Main St. (5th St.) | 707-259-0762 | www.napageneralstore.com

This combo gift shop/gourmet food store and cafe in a "rustic" historic mill building offers "delicious" prepared food for picnics, plus breakfast and lunch - the latter featuring "relatively reasonably" priced Cal-Eclectic entrees like Chinese chicken salad; consider sitting out on the patio with its "mosaic mural" and view of the Napa River; N.B. the kitchen closes at 5 PM Monday–Sunday.

**Napa Valley Grille** *Californian* 20 20 20 $42

**Yountville** | Washington Sq. | 6795 Washington St. (off Hwy. 29) | 707-944-8686 | www.napavalleygrille.com

A "local fave", this "consistent", long-standing Californian in Yountville is "nice all-around" note fans of its "bistro-style" dishes including a "Kobe beef burger"; it's "open throughout the afternoon", so if you're looking for a "late lunch or early dinner" on an outdoor patio with a view of the vineyards, washed down with a bottle from the "excellent wine selection", you're in luck.

**Napa Valley Wine Train** *Californian* 17 22 19 $67

**Napa** | 1275 McKinstry St. (bet. 1st St. & Soscol Ave.) | 707-253-2111 | www.winetrain.com

"You have to do this at least once" enthuse railway buffs who tout the "incomparable" experience of "enjoying a gourmet meal" of Cal cuisine paired with local wines and "beautiful views of the valley" as you "click-clack" along in a "historic train" chugging north from Napa; but some who aren't on board beef about the "so-so" food that's not worth the "astronomical" price.

**955 Ukiah** 🄼 *American/French* ▽ 21 20 23 $44

**Mendocino** | 955 Ukiah St. (School St.) | 707-937-1955 | www.955restaurant.com

For a "classic North Coast" experience, this family-run, art-filled Mendocino Village "hideaway" tucked down a garden path remains a neighborhood "favorite" for "straightforward" locally sourced food and wine; the New American-French menu may "read like all of the others" in town and the interior may hark back to the "'70s", but the "reasonable" prices, "delicious" fare and "totally unpretentious" crew make up for it; N.B. open for dinner only Thursday–Sunday.

**NEW Odyssey** Ⓢ Ⓜ *American* ▽ 19 | 13 | 18 | $45

**Windsor** | 426 Emily Rose Circle (off Hwy. 101) | 707-836-7600 | www.odyssey-restaurant.com

Considering chef Rudy Mihal once worked at Manhattan's Gramercy Tavern, it's no wonder this "tiny" space is like "a little piece of New York in Windsor"; the "limited menu" is "strong" on "epic portions" of "imaginative" Italian- and French-accented American dishes; too bad the "cramped" quarters can get "really loud" ("avoid weekends if you want to hear your companion"), because it's an "intimate" option with an "eclectic, interesting wine list."

**Osake** Ⓢ *Californian/Japanese* 23 | 16 | 19 | $36

**Santa Rosa** | 2446 Patio Ct. (Farmers Ln.) | 707-542-8282

**Sake 'O** Ⓜ *Californian/Japanese*

**Healdsburg** | 505 Healdsburg Ave. (Piper St.) | 707-433-2669 www.garychus.com

"It's always fun to see owner Gary Chu" at this pair of Cal-Japanese cousins in Santa Rosa and Healdsburg, watching him "greet customers" and "whip up" "inventive sushi" and "specialties" like martini prawns; despite the "uninspired" location of the Patio Court original (it's "tucked away in a strip mall") and service that's sometimes "slow", fin-atics are "always pleased" with the "fresh" fare.

**NEW Oxbow Wine Merchant** *Californian/Mediterranean* - | - | - | M

**Napa** | Oxbow Public Mkt. | 610 First St. (east of Soscol Ave.) | 707-257-5200 | www.fpwm.com

Oxbow Public Market's new retail shop and wine bar hawks Cal-Med bites (think charcuterie plates and mac 'n' cheese), over 100 types of *fromage* and *beaucoup* boutique domestic and imported pours, available by the taste, glass, carafe and bottle; as for seating, there's a 30-seat square bar in the center of the store, plus patio tables overlooking the Napa River; N.B. there's a $6 corkage for anything off the shelf.

**Pangaea** Ⓜ *Californian/French* ▽ 19 | 17 | 19 | $46

**Gualala** | 39165 S. Hwy. 1 (east side of the hwy.) | 707-884-9669 | www.pangaeacafe.com

A "nice little place to stop" on your way up Highway 1 is this "creative" Californian-French charmer whose "lusty cooking" is inspired by the "bounty of Mendocino's gardens and waters" (much of the "fresh" food comes from a 20-mile radius, and the "excellent" wine list features many biodynamic bottles); though the space is "small", "if the weather's right", you can "eat outside"; N.B. open Wednesday-Sunday only.

**NEW Peter Lowell's** *Italian* | - | - | - | M |

**Sebastopol** | 7385 Healdsburg Ave., Ste. 101 (Florence Ave.) | 707-829-1077 | www.peterlowells.com

This "crunchy" yet "stylish" all-day Sebastopol cafe hawks "nicely done", "Italian-inspired, primarily plant-based" organic eats in a certified green storefront quickly becoming a "new favorite" among the "local trust-fund hippies"; order deli-style from the PaperStone bar by day or enjoy "friendly" table service at night, when the "limited" evening specials (including seafood and meat options) are complemented by "carefully chosen" biodynamic wines.

**Pica Pica Maize Kitchen** *S American* | - | - | - | I |

**Napa** | Oxbow Public Mkt. | 610 First St. (McKinstry St.) | 707-251-3757 | www.picapicakitchen.com

This little Venezuelan in Downtown Napa's new Oxbow Public Market showcases corn-centric cuisine, including arepas filled with everything from steak and black beans to tofu and vegetables, plus 'Maize'wiches' (grilled cheese on cornbread), fried plantains, yuca fries and salads; bottled beers and housemade South American beverages like coconut lemonade round out the offerings, all of which can be savored in the food court or on the patio overlooking the river.

**Pizzeria Tra Vigne** *Pizza* | 21 | 17 | 17 | $25 |

**St. Helena** | Inn at Southbridge | 1016 Main St. (Pope St.) | 707-967-9999 | www.travignerestaurant.com

"Perfect" "when you want a break from oh-so-rich food on a wine country weekend" - and "just about the only place to take kids" without spending loads of "dough" declare St. Helenans who congregate at the Inn at Southbridge's pizzeria; service can be "frustrating", but few mind because the Neapolitan crusts and salads are topped with "what the good earth in Napa has to offer", while the "big-screen TV, pool table" and patio ensure there's "never a dull moment."

**Press** *American/Steak* 22 | 25 | 22 | $76

**St. Helena** | 587 St. Helena Hwy. (White Ln.) | 707-967-0550 | www.pressthelena.com

Giving "carnivores reason to celebrate", this St. Helena American steakhouse doles out "big portions" of "beef like butter", some of it "carved at the table"; its "stunningly modern space" - "chic and stylish, yet not cold or sterile" - "lively bar scene" and "encyclopedic" "list of local wines" keep the "steak, steak, steak"-lovers "coming back again and again", even if some say service is "hit-or-miss" and penny pinchers posit it's "pricey for what you get."

**Ravenous Cafe** Ⓜ *Californian/Eclectic* 22 | 17 | 17 | $42

**Healdsburg** | 420 Center St. (North St.) | 707-431-1302

For "hearty", "casual" Cal-Electic cuisine, Healdsburg habitués hoof it to this "informal", "funky old cottage" done up in "Home Depot orange", where the "upscale home cooking" includes "awesome" burgers and "innovative", "underpriced" entrees; the "tree-covered patio" is "lovely" on "gorgeous summer evenings", though locals know to avoid the "slow" service by grabbing a seat inside at the bar, where the bartenders have an "impressive" knowledge of the wine list.

**Ravens Restaurant, The** *Vegan* ∇ 20 | 20 | 19 | $47

**Mendocino** | Stanford Inn & Spa | Coast Hwy. & Comptche Ukiah Rd. (Hwy. 1) | 707-937-5615 | www.stanfordinn.com

"Unique" "high-style vegan food", paired with organic and biodynamic wines, prompts even omnivores to consider this veggie haven "worth another visit"; the "serene setting" in Mendocino's Stanford Inn with "spectacular views" of the bay and gardens helps soften the "expensive" prices, yet a few doubters find the fare "uninspired", asking if it might be "too healthy for its own good"; N.B. breakfast and dinner only.

**Z Redd Restaurant** *Californian* 27 | 22 | 24 | $73

**Yountville** | 6480 Washington St. (California Dr.) | 707-944-2222 | www.reddnapavalley.com

A "modern Californian-cuisine genius", chef-owner Richard Reddington "aims to please" and hits his target at this "special place in a town full of special places", Yountville; "from fish to fowl to filet", "every dish is a work of art" say Redd-blooded reviewers, who are "impressed with everything" from the "cutting-edge" menu and "ambitious" wine list to the "sophisticated" "minimalist" (some say "stark") setting; a "top-notch" sommelier and "gracious" servers even manage "to make the expensive tab seem reasonable."

**Rendezvous Inn & Restaurant** Ⓜ *French* ▽ 25 | 19 | 22 | $51

**Fort Bragg** | 647 N. Main St. (Bush St.) | 707-964-8142 | www.rendezvousinn.com

Although this "wonderful find" is a "little way out of Mendocino", it's "definitely worth" a rendezvous to "down-to-earth Fort Bragg"; Kim Badenhop was "trained in France and it shows" in his "carefully" crafted, seasonally driven New French fare "cooked to perfection"; dining in the "turn-of-the-century" Craftsman-style B&B with redwood paneling and a fireplace is "like eating in someone's very gracious home" – the staff is "attentive" and the chef even "visits each table, ensuring that guests enjoy their meals."

**Restaurant, The** *American/Eclectic* ▽ 22 | 17 | 22 | $42

**Fort Bragg** | 418 N. Main St. (Laurel St.) | 707-964-9800 | www.therestaurantfortbragg.com

Chef-owner James Larsen has been concocting "consistently good" food in his "funky, warm little eatery for decades", giving Fort Bragg residents somewhere to "send visitors for a bit of local color" since 1973; the "well-thought-out" New American-Eclectic menu and the "marvelous" (if occasionally "morbid") paintings by local artist Olaf Palm throughout inspire conversation, which helps explain why this "institution on Main Street" is an area "favorite."

**Restaurant at Stevenswood, The** *Mediterranean* ▽ 25 | 24 | 23 | $57

**Little River** | Stevenswood Lodge | 8211 Shoreline Hwy./N. Hwy. 1 (1.5 minutes south of Mendocino) | 707-937-2810 | www.stevenswood.com

A "hidden treasure" just south of Mendocino in Little River, this "charming" spot in the Stevenswood Lodge serves "sophisticated" Mediterranean meals under "creative new chef" Patrick Meaney; surrounded by the towering redwoods of Van Damme State Park, it has a "fine setting in the trees" with "a view of the garden" from the "intimate" dining room equipped with a working fireplace; P.S. there are also "great breakfasts."

| | FOOD | DECOR | SERVICE | COST |
|---|---|---|---|---|

**NEW Risibisi** *Italian* ▽ 21 | 19 | 17 | $42

**Petaluma** | 154 Petaluma Blvd. N. (Washington St.) | 707-766-7600 | www.risibisirestaurant.com

"Enjoy a glass of bubbly" in the "lovely" back room before tucking into the "high-quality" Northern Italian fare at this "exciting newcomer" recommend romantics who fancy it a "sophisticated" "date spot" and "one of the few places in Petaluma you don't feel silly dressing up"; the Venetian "slow food" is "delicious", but surveyors are split on service that ranges from "so fabulous you want to hug them" to "you never want to see them again."

**NEW Rôtisario** *BBQ* - | - | - | I

**Napa** | Oxbow Public Mkt. | 610 First St. (McKinstry St.) | 510-780-0300 | www.roliroti.com

The "best deal in town" for "healthy, delish" dishes may come from this all-day, counter-service outpost of Roli Roti specializing in "delicious" rotisserie chicken, tri-tip, meatloaf and, on Saturdays and Sundays only, pork; the meats are all served as a sandwich or on a combo plate (with roasted or Frenched potatoes and "farm fresh" salad) "to take home" or eat in at the eight-seat bar or riverfront patio in Napa's Oxbow Market.

**Rutherford Grill** *American* 23 | 19 | 21 | $38

**Rutherford** | 1180 Rutherford Rd. (Hwy. 29) | 707-963-1792 | www.hillstone.com

"Hearty portions" of "unpretentious" "all-American" eats, "friendly and efficient" service, "reasonable prices" and a "no-corkage" policy that encourages diners to bring "something they discovered while wine tasting" keep this Rutherford sibling of the Houston's chain "always crowded"; some call the patio "Napa's version of a singles bar", where you can lounge by the "outdoor fire" with a crowd consisting largely of "locals."

**Santé** *Californian/French* ▽ 24 | 21 | 24 | $64

**Sonoma** | Fairmont Sonoma Mission Inn & Spa | 100 Boyes Blvd. (Sonoma Hwy.) | 707-939-2415 | www.fairmont.com

"My favorite place to drive to – wish I had a mistress to take along" jest habitués who make tracks to this "wonderful" Californian with French influences that's "definitely up to the quality" of the "elegant, but not stuffy" Fairmont Sonoma Mission Inn; the "well-thought-out" fare is "nicely executed", the wine list "excellent", the "engaging" "staff makes dining enjoyable" and with the resort right there, there's "no need to leave"; still, a handful huff it's "not as memorable as the bill would have me believe."

**Santi** *Italian* 24 | 18 | 21 | $48

**Geyserville** | 21047 Geyserville Ave. (Hwy. 128) | 707-857-1790 | www.tavernasanti.com

One of the "best-kept secrets" in "wine country" according to *amici*, this "delightful" destination is "worth the drive" to "tiny", "out-of-the-way" Geyserville for its "homey", "*squisito*" Northern Italian cuisine and selection of "local" wines, served by an "attentive" staff; "on a nice evening" (which is almost "all the time in Sonoma"), ask for "a table on the patio", although many enjoy the "warm and cozy" interior as well.

**Sharon's By the Sea** *Italian/Seafood* ∇ 18 | 13 | 17 | $35

**Fort Bragg** | Noyo Harbor | 32096 N. Harbor Dr. (Hwy. 1) | 707-962-0680 | www.sharonsbythesea.com

For "always satisfying" Italian seafood accompanied by Mendo wines, locals pronounce this "wonderful find" right on "the Fort Bragg wharf" by the Noyo Bridge "the place to go"; "scarf down" "standout dishes" like seasonal crab Louie made with crustaceans plucked "straight from waters outside the door" of the "cozy", "kitschy" "tight" quarters or sit outside and "watch the Coastguard tugs enter the harbor."

**Sooze Wine Bar Café** 🅼 *Californian* ∇ 25 | 17 | 24 | $40

**Petaluma** | Great Petaluma Mill | 6 Petaluma Blvd. N. (B St.) | 707-762-3743

"A great chef and host", owner Soo Young Kim "does an excellent job of steering you to the perfect wines for your palate" at this "arty but unassuming little place" inside the Great Petaluma Mill that offers an "unparalleled by-the-glass list" and a "level of cooking to match" on its midpriced menu of Californian cuisine; with only 24 seats indoors and eight out, it's also an "intimate" spot for a "romantic" rendezvous.

**St. Orres** *Californian* ∇ 22 | 26 | 22 | $65

**Gualala** | 36601 S. Hwy. 1 (2 mi. north of Gualala) | 707-884-3303 | www.saintorres.com

Chef-owner Rosemary Campiformio "understands native Californian cuisine" say admirers of her "creative" and "wonderful prix fixe menu" featuring "exotic mushrooms, wild game" and "unique Pacific seafood"; the "romantic", "rustic" Russian-style dining room - under a three-story onion dome - "feels like a true escape", making it "worth the long drive" to the "beautiful" St. Orres Bed & Breakfast, a few miles north of Gualala.

**Syrah** *Californian/French* 25 | 18 | 23 | $48

**Santa Rosa** | 205 Fifth St. (Davis St.) | 707-568-4002 | www.syrahbistro.com

This "real find" in Santa Rosa's Railroad Square is where chef/co-owner "Josh Silver continues to rock the house"; "trust the chef's choices" by ordering the "wonderful tasting menu" crafted from "local products done perfectly" or order à la carte from the "ever-changing" "seasonal" Cal-French menu that "keeps this gem intriguing"; "knowledgeable" and "attentive but not hovering" staffers are "sure to please", even if the decor is deemed "a bit industrial" by some.

**Taylor's Automatic Refresher** *Diner* 21 | 13 | 14 | $17

NEW **Napa** | Oxbow Public Mkt. | 644 First St. (McKinstry St.) | 707-224-6900

**St. Helena** | 933 Main St. (bet. Charter Oak Ave. & Pope St.) | 707-963-3486

www.taylorsrefresher.com

"Possibly the only drive-in in America with a corkage fee", this "wine-country version of a 1950s diner" hawks "bottles of Opus" alongside "American favorites" like fries, "four-star hamburgers" and "killer ahi tacos"; the "picnic table"-only St. Helena flagship (which spawned the "larger" Napa Oxbow Market and SF Ferry Building sit-down sibs) would "be a real 'refresher' if tour buses didn't make an 'automatic' stop", resulting in "insane lines."

Z **Terra** *American* 26 | 23 | 23 | $69

**St. Helena** | 1345 Railroad Ave. (bet. Adams St. & Hunt Ave.) | 707-963-8931 | www.terrarestaurant.com

"Hiro's a hero" chant champions of chef Hiro Sone and his pastry-whiz wife Lissa Doumani's "elegant" St. Helena Asian-accented New American that "sparks the taste buds" with "dreamy", "perfectly executed" dishes and a "wonderful wine list"; its fieldstone-lined space is "lovely", and while some say the mostly "polished service" can be "unfriendly", all in all, the experience is "as romantic as it can get" for fawners who "fall in love all over again every time" they visit.

**Tra Vigne** *Italian* 23 | 24 | 22 | $55

**St. Helena** | 1050 Charter Oak Ave. (Hwy. 29) | 707-963-4444 | www.travignerestaurant.com

"Thanks to chef Nash Cognetti", this St. Helena "stalwart" has "gotten its groove back" say the majority of surveyors, who note its Northern Italian fare is once again "worthy of the venue" - "one of the prettiest rooms in town" and an "idyllic" courtyard where the "dappled sunlight" and "soothing fountain" make you "swear you're in Tuscany"; "to give your palate the best possible experience", "ask for suggestions" and wine pairings from the "well-educated" servers.

**NEW 25º Brix Restaurant & Gardens** *Californian/Mediterranean* - | - | - | M

**Napa** | 7377 St. Helena Hwy. (Yount Mill Rd.) | 707-944-2749 | www.25degreesbrix.com

SF restaurateur David Gingrass (TWO) has teamed with the original owners of Napa Valley's Brix to reinvent it as a modern-day farmhouse serving midpriced Cal-Med fare; guests can stroll the on-site gardens and vineyards before sitting down to enjoy the new farm-to-table menu, then retire to the outdoor terrace overlooking the Mayacamas Mountains or swing by the wine shop to pick up a bottle to go.

**Ubuntu** *Californian/Vegan* 24 | 25 | 22 | $43

**Napa** | 1140 Main St. (Pearl St.) | 707-251-5656 | www.ubuntunapa.com

"Good for you and for the planet", this "hip" Downtown Napa newcomer is the "perfect place" to "align your food chakra" by dining on "mind-blowing" Californian meat-free cuisine "like it's never been done before", which chef Jeremy Fox (ex Manresa) sources in part from the restaurant's biodynamic gardens; "interesting" sustainable wines, "Zen-based" service and an "open loft" setting that affords "silhouette" views of the "synchronized postures of yoga students upstairs" all add up to a "totally different" vegetarian dining experience.

**Underwood Bar & Bistro** M *Mediterranean* 23 | 20 | 18 | $42

**Graton** | 9113 Graton Rd. (Edison St.) | 707-823-7023 | www.underwoodgraton.com

Perhaps the "closest thing" to a "happening San Francisco scene" in "Podunk" Graton, this "country-yuppie" place is "worth seeking out" for "excellent" Mediterranean tapas, "oysters and special entrees" "after a day of vino tasting"; dark wood and frosted glass create an "urban feel", as do the "noisy" "crowds-beyond-belief for dinner" - so either "bring a megaphone" or just "give your table to someone else and stay at the bar" to revel in "spectacular cocktails and knowledgeable wine service" or try your hand on the bocce ball court.

**Uva Trattoria & Bar** M *Italian* ∇ 23 | 20 | 22 | $39

**Napa** | 1040 Clinton St. (bet. Brown & Main Sts.) | 707-255-6646 | www.uvatrattoria.com

Whether for "a sit-down dinner" or "nibbling" at the "busy bar" with a wine from the "extensive" list, this "hopping" Napa Italian "pleases any palate" with the "amazing" "fresh" fare from chef Giovanni Guerrera; add in "live music" (Wednesday-Sunday with no cover) and staffers who "make you feel like family" and it explains why it's a "favorite of locals."

**Wappo Bar Bistro** *Eclectic* ∇ 22 | 18 | 19 | $44

**Calistoga** | 1226 Washington St. (Lincoln Ave.) | 707-942-4712 | www.wappobar.com

"In a town where restaurants come and go, it's no wonder" this "Calistoga standby" has "been here for so long", as the "ambitious", often "ingenious", "very Eclectic" global comfort food, augmented by "delicious wines you don't see everywhere", continues to "surprise"; although the atmosphere in the redwood-bedecked interior is "quite good", the "delightfully landscaped patio", "blazing with colors" and topped by a grapevine-covered arbor, is "too inviting not to eat on."

**Water Street Bistro** ⊄ *French* ∇ 25 | 17 | 19 | $22

**Petaluma** | 100 Petaluma Blvd. N. (Western Ave.) | 707-763-9563

On "balmy afternoons" the best seats are "out on the patio" "overlooking the Petaluma River" at this tiny "waterfront" French bistro; the "personable" chef-owner has a "sure hand" with "beautifully prepared" affordable fare including "creative" "soups and sandwiches"; but "slow" service sometimes suggests "they need more help"; N.B. breakfast and lunch only, and monthly theme dinners by reservation.

**Willi's Seafood & Raw Bar** *Seafood* 23 | 19 | 20 | $42

**Healdsburg** | 403 Healdsburg Ave. (North St.) | 707-433-9191 | www.willisseafood.net

The "wonderful" raw bar bites and "creative" tapas "couldn't get much fresher" at this "high-energy" Healdsburg "seafood specialist" where "it's always a treat" to "sit outside" on the "convivial" patio" and "people-watch"; sure, the tabs on those "small plates" "add up fast" but rather than "get crabby", supporters just order a "very cool cocktail" or one of the "many wines by the glass."

**Willi's Wine Bar** *Eclectic* 25 | 19 | 22 | $46

**Santa Rosa** | Orchard Inn | 4404 Old Redwood Hwy. (Ursuline Rd.) | 707-526-3096 | www.williswinebar.net

"Go with friends" so you'll have "ample opportunity to sample" many of the "absolutely knockout" nibbles at this "titillating" Electic eatery, "the crown jewel in the Stark empire"; the "charming roadhouse" with "patio dining is so pleasant" it hardly seems like "you're just off the highway" in Santa Rosa rave regulars, who "join the winemakers" "running up a sizable tab" "sampling local" vintages from the "ever-changing wines-by-the-glass list."

**Willow Wood Market Cafe** *Eclectic/Mediterranean* 23 | 19 | 18 | $27

**Graton** | 9020 Graton Rd. (Brush St.) | 707-823-0233 | www.willowwoodgraton.com

"Wine biz folks" and tourists alike "drive quite a way" on Russian River "expeditions" to this "consistently charming", "quirky cafe" in the "middle-of-nowhere" town of Graton for the "ultimate" Eclectic-Med "comfort food" with American influences; brunch is "worth getting out of bed for", though afterwards, you "feel like the big fat bumblebees who buzz languidly on the back porch"; "service is often slower than molasses", so check out the "doodads" in the General Store "while waiting for a table."

**Wine Spectator Greystone** *Californian* 22 | 23 | 22 | $54

**St. Helena** | Culinary Institute of America | 2555 Main St. (Deer Park Rd.) | 707-967-1010 | www.ciachef.edu

"Check out the action" in the "very open kitchen", or "drink in the view" from the patio "overlooking the valley" and the grounds of the Culinary Institute of America, St. Helena's renowned "training ground" for chefs 1; it's a "very romantic setting" for the sometimes "plate-lickin' good" Californian-Eclectic cuisine; the "expansive room" is a "tad loud" and definitely "touristy", but the servers "try to please" so it can add up to an "extraordinary culinary experience."

| | FOOD | DECOR | SERVICE | COST |
|---|---|---|---|---|
| **zazu** [M] *American/Italian* | 24 | 17 | 22 | $46 |

**Santa Rosa** | 3535 Guerneville Rd. (Willowside Rd.) | 707-523-4814 | www.zazurestaurant.com

"The casual roadhouse atmosphere is part of the charm" at this "funky and fabulous" "local favorite" "in the middle of nowhere" on the outskirts of Santa Rosa that the green-thumbed call "a gardener's dream" for its "ever-changing" New American–Northern Italian menu full of "produce and herbs picked fresh" from the plot out back; it's "heaven in the sticks" opine oenophiles, who "glow" after a few glasses of the "reasonably priced local wines" and recommend the "great Pizza & Pinot nights."

| | FOOD | DECOR | SERVICE | COST |
|---|---|---|---|---|
| **Zin** *American* | 22 | 18 | 20 | $42 |

**Healdsburg** | 344 Center St. (North St.) | 707-473-0946 | www.zinrestaurant.com

This "blue-plate" paradise is a "perennial favorite" with Healdsburg habitués, including "many a winemaker" who appreciate the "home-style" New American menu and "daily specials"; ask a "very accommodating" server to "help you pick the perfect wine" – "they have tons of zins" – and don't forget beer-battered green beans, which are "on almost every table"; though a few feel it lacks zing, most call it a "solid" spot.

| | FOOD | DECOR | SERVICE | COST |
|---|---|---|---|---|
| **Zinsvalley** [S] *American* | ∇ 20 | 18 | 18 | $37 |

**Napa** | Browns Valley Shopping Ctr. | 3253 Browns Valley Rd. (bet. Austin & Larkin Sts.) | 707-224-0695 | www.zinsvalley.com

"Loved by locals and visitors lucky enough to have found it", this "haunt" with a "friendly" vibe and two fireplaces "tucked away in a Napa" market center well off Highway 29 serves up "simple but tasty" New American fare in "lovely surroundings"; the "cozy" digs include a "patio next to the creek" and a fountain – what a "nice place" to "enjoy some Zin"; N.B. there's free corkage for two bottles.

| | FOOD | DECOR | SERVICE | COST |
|---|---|---|---|---|
| **ZuZu** *Spanish* | 24 | 18 | 20 | $42 |

**Napa** | 829 Main St. (bet. 2nd & 3rd Sts.) | 707-224-8555 | www.zuzunapa.com

"Each plate is a little masterpiece" at this "friendly" Spanish "small plates paradise", a candle-lit Napa tapa "fave" where the menu "changes with the season" and the "wines are picked perfectly"; the "informal" food is "great for late-night dining", but "be prepared to wait", because it's "always busy" and there are "no reservations."

# Cuisines

Includes restaurant names, locations and Food ratings. Z indicates places with the highest ratings, popularity and importance.

## AMERICAN (NEW)

| | |
|---|---|
| Z Cafe La Haye \| **Sonoma** | 26 |
| Celadon \| **Napa** | 24 |
| Cindy's \| **St. Helena** | 24 |
| Deuce \| **Sonoma** | 22 |
| Dry Creek \| **Healdsburg** | 24 |
| Duck Club \| **Bodega** | 20 |
| Farm \| **Napa** | 25 |
| Z French Laundry \| **Yountville** | 29 |
| Fumé Bistro \| **Napa** | 21 |
| NEW JoLe \| **Calistoga** | - |
| Kenwood \| **Kenwood** | 23 |
| Madrona Manor \| **Healdsburg** | 26 |
| Z Martini House \| **St. Helena** | 26 |
| Mendo Bistro \| **Ft Bragg** | 24 |
| Monti's \| **Santa Rosa** | 20 |
| Mustards Grill \| **Yountville** | 24 |
| 955 Ukiah \| **Mendocino** | 21 |
| NEW Odyssey \| **Windsor** | 19 |
| Restaurant, The \| **Ft Bragg** | 22 |
| Z Terra \| **St. Helena** | 26 |
| zazu \| **Santa Rosa** | 24 |
| Zin \| **Healdsburg** | 22 |
| Zinsvalley \| **Napa** | 20 |

## AMERICAN (TRADITIONAL)

| | |
|---|---|
| Z Ad Hoc \| **Yountville** | 26 |
| Barndiva \| **Healdsburg** | 18 |
| Brannan's Grill \| **Calistoga** | 20 |
| Chapter & Moon \| **Ft Bragg** | 20 |
| Cuvée \| **Napa** | 20 |
| Foothill Grille \| **Napa** | 20 |
| NEW Healdsburg B&G \| **Healdsburg** | - |
| In-N-Out \| **Napa** | 21 |
| Market \| **St. Helena** | 22 |
| Press \| **St. Helena** | 22 |
| Rutherford Grill \| **Rutherford** | 23 |
| Taylor's Auto \| **Napa** | 21 |

## BAKERIES

| | |
|---|---|
| Alexis Baking Co. \| **Napa** | 22 |
| Della Fattoria \| **Petaluma** | 25 |
| Downtown Bakery \| **Healdsburg** | 22 |
| Model Bakery \| **multi.** | 20 |

## BARBECUE

| | |
|---|---|
| NEW BarBersQ \| **Napa** | 22 |
| Bounty Hunter \| **Napa** | 17 |
| NEW Rôtisario \| **Napa** | - |

## BRITISH

| | |
|---|---|
| Betty's Fish \| **Santa Rosa** | 20 |

## BURGERS

| | |
|---|---|
| NEW Healdsburg B&G \| **Healdsburg** | - |
| In-N-Out \| **Napa** | 21 |
| Taylor's Auto \| **multi.** | 21 |

## CALIFORNIAN

| | |
|---|---|
| Albion River Inn \| **Albion** | 22 |
| All Seasons \| **Calistoga** | 21 |
| Applewood Inn \| **Guerneville** | 24 |
| Auberge du Sol. \| **Rutherford** | 25 |
| Bistro Ralph \| **Healdsburg** | 22 |
| Boon Fly Café \| **Napa** | 21 |
| Boonville Hotel \| **Boonville** | 22 |
| Cafe Beaujolais \| **Mendocino** | 25 |
| Z Cafe La Haye \| **Sonoma** | 26 |
| Carneros Bistro \| **Sonoma** | 20 |
| Central Market \| **Petaluma** | 23 |
| Cindy's \| **St. Helena** | 24 |
| El Dorado \| **Sonoma** | 21 |
| Étoile \| **Yountville** | 25 |

Farmhouse Inn | **Forestville** 26
Flavor | **Santa Rosa** 20
NEW Folio Enoteca | **Napa** 23
Hurley's | **Yountville** 17
John Ash & Co. | **Santa Rosa** 23
Julia's | **Napa** 23
Ledford Hse. | **Albion** 24
Little River Inn | **Little River** 22
MacCallum Hse. | **Mendocino** 23
Manzanita | **Healdsburg** 20
Meadowood Grill | **St. Helena** 20
Z Meadowood Rest. | **St. Helena** 26
Mendocino Hotel | **Mendocino** 18
Moosse Café | **Mendocino** 23
Mosaic | **Forestville** 26
Mustards Grill | **Yountville** 24
Napa General Store | **Napa** 19
Napa Valley Grille | **Yountville** 20
Napa Wine Train | **Napa** 17
Osake/Sake 'O | **Santa Rosa** 23
NEW Oxbow Wine | **Napa** -
Pangaea | **Gualala** 19
Ravenous Cafe | **Healdsburg** 22
Z Redd | **Yountville** 27
Santé | **Sonoma** 24
Sooze Wine | **Petaluma** 25
St. Orres | **Gualala** 22
Syrah | **Santa Rosa** 25
NEW 25º Brix | **Napa** -
Ubuntu | **Napa** 24
Wine Spectator | **St. Helena** 22

## CHINESE

Gary Chu's | **Santa Rosa** 21

## COFFEE SHOPS/DINERS

Taylor's Auto | **multi.** 21

## DELIS

Jimtown Store | **Healdsburg** 18

## DESSERT

Model Bakery | **multi.** 20

## ECLECTIC

Celadon | **Napa** 24
Della Fattoria | **Petaluma** 25
Flavor | **Santa Rosa** 20
Go Fish | **St. Helena** 23
NEW Hopmonk Tav. | **Sebastopol** -
Napa General Store | **Napa** 19
Ravenous Cafe | **Healdsburg** 22
Restaurant, The | **Ft Bragg** 22
Wappo Bar | **Calistoga** 22
Willi's Wine | **Santa Rosa** 25
Willow Wood | **Graton** 23
Wine Spectator | **St. Helena** 22

## FRENCH

Angèle | **Napa** 22
Auberge du Sol. | **Rutherford** 25
Bistro/Copains | **Occidental/N** 26
Brannan's Grill | **Calistoga** 20
Cafe Beaujolais | **Mendocino** 25
Z Cyrus | **Healdsburg** 29
fig cafe | **Glen Ellen** 23
Z French Laundry | **Yountville** 29
Julia's | **Napa** 23
Kenwood | **Kenwood** 23
La Toque | **Napa** 26
Madrona Manor | **Healdsburg** 26
955 Ukiah | **Mendocino** 21
Pangaea | **Gualala** 19
Rendezvous Inn | **Ft Bragg** 25
Santé | **Sonoma** 24

## FRENCH (BISTRO)

Z Bistro Jeanty | **Yountville** 26
Bistro Ralph | **Healdsburg** 22
Bouchon | **Yountville** 26
Charcuterie | **Healdsburg** 23
girl & the fig | **Sonoma** 23
K&L Bistro | **Sebastopol** 24
Mirepoix | **Windsor** 25
Syrah | **Santa Rosa** 25
Water St. Bistro | **Petaluma** 25

## ITALIAN

(N=Northern; S=Southern)

- Azzurro Pizzeria | **Napa** 23
- Bistro Don Giovanni | **Napa** 23
- Bovolo | **Healdsburg** 22
- Cafe Citti | N | **Kenwood** 22
- Cook St. Helena | N | **St. Helena** 24
- Cucina Paradiso | S | **Petaluma** 24
- Della Santina's | N | **Sonoma** 20
- **NEW** Diavola | **Geyserville** -
- Meritage Martini | N | **Sonoma** 20
- **NEW** Peter Lowell's | **Sebastopol** -
- Pizzeria Tra Vigne | **St. Helena** 21
- **NEW** Risibisi | N | **Petaluma** 21
- Santi | N | **Geyserville** 24
- Sharon's | **Ft Bragg** 18
- Tra Vigne | N | **St. Helena** 23
- Uva Trattoria | **Napa** 23
- zazu | N | **Santa Rosa** 24

## JAPANESE

(* sushi specialist)

- **Z** Hana Japanese* | **Rohnert Pk** 26
- Osake/Sake 'O'* | **multi.** 23

## MEDITERRANEAN

- Central Market | **Petaluma** 23
- El Dorado | **Sonoma** 21
- **NEW** Folio Enoteca | **Napa** 23
- Hurley's | **Yountville** 17
- Ledford Hse. | **Albion** 24
- Manzanita | **Healdsburg** 20
- Monti's | **Santa Rosa** 20
- **NEW** Oxbow Wine | **Napa** -
- Rest. at Stevenswood | **Little River** 25
- **NEW** 25º Brix | **Napa** -
- Underwood Bar | **Graton** 23
- Willow Wood | **Graton** 23

## PIZZA

- Azzurro Pizzeria | **Napa** 23
- **NEW** Diavola | **Geyserville** -
- Pizzeria Tra Vigne | **St. Helena** 21

## PORTUGUESE

- LaSalette | **Sonoma** 22

## SANDWICHES

- Downtown Bakery | **Healdsburg** 22
- Jimtown Store | **Healdsburg** 18
- Model Bakery | **multi.** 20

## SEAFOOD

- Go Fish | **St. Helena** 23
- Little River Inn | **Little River** 22
- Meritage Martini | **Sonoma** 20
- Sharon's | **Ft Bragg** 18
- Willi's Seafood | **Healdsburg** 23

## SMALL PLATES

(See also Spanish tapas specialist)

- **NEW** JoLe | Amer. | **Calistoga** -
- Monti's | Med. | **Santa Rosa** 20
- **NEW** Oxbow Wine | Amer. | **Napa** -
- Underwood Bar | Med. | **Graton** 23
- Willi's Seafood | Seafood | **Healdsburg** 23
- Willi's Wine | Eclectic | **Santa Rosa** 25

## SPANISH

(* tapas specialist)

- ZuZu* | **Napa** 24

## STEAKHOUSES

- Cole's Chop Hse. | **Napa** 24
- Press | **St. Helena** 22

## VEGETARIAN

(* vegan)

- Ravens Rest.* | **Mendocino** 20
- Ubuntu* | **Napa** 24

## VENEZUELAN

- Pica Pica Maize | **Napa** -

## VIETNAMESE

- Annalien | **Napa** 24

# Locations

Includes restaurant names, cuisines and Food ratings. ☒ indicates places with the highest Food ratings.

## Mendocino

### ALBION

| | | |
|---|---|---|
| Albion River Inn | *Cal.* | 22 |
| Ledford Hse. | *Cal./Med.* | 24 |

### BOONVILLE

| | | |
|---|---|---|
| Boonville Hotel | *Cal.* | 22 |

### FORT BRAGG

| | | |
|---|---|---|
| Chapter & Moon | *Amer.* | 20 |
| Mendo Bistro | *Amer.* | 24 |
| Rendezvous Inn | *French* | 25 |
| Restaurant, The | *Amer./Eclectic* | 22 |
| Sharon's | *Italian/Seafood* | 18 |

### GUALALA

| | | |
|---|---|---|
| Pangaea | *Cal./French* | 19 |
| St. Orres | *Cal.* | 22 |

### LITTLE RIVER

| | | |
|---|---|---|
| Little River Inn | *Cal./Seafood* | 22 |
| Rest. at Stevenswood | *Med.* | 25 |

### MENDOCINO

| | | |
|---|---|---|
| Cafe Beaujolais | *Cal./French* | 25 |
| MacCallum Hse. | *Cal.* | 23 |
| Mendocino Hotel | *Cal.* | 18 |
| Moosse Café | *Cal.* | 23 |
| 955 Ukiah | *Amer./French* | 21 |
| Ravens Rest. | *Vegan* | 20 |

## Napa

### CALISTOGA

| | | |
|---|---|---|
| All Seasons | *Cal.* | 21 |
| Brannan's Grill | *Amer./French* | 20 |
| NEW JoLe | *Amer.* | - |
| Wappo Bar | *Eclectic* | 22 |

### NAPA

| | | |
|---|---|---|
| Alexis Baking Co. | *Bakery* | 22 |
| Angèle | *French* | 22 |
| Annalien | *Viet.* | 24 |
| Azzurro Pizzeria | *Pizza* | 23 |
| NEW BarBersQ | *BBQ* | 22 |
| Bistro Don Giovanni | *Italian* | 23 |
| Boon Fly Café | *Cal.* | 21 |
| Bounty Hunter | *BBQ* | 17 |
| Celadon | *Amer./Eclectic* | 24 |
| Cole's Chop Hse. | *Steak* | 24 |
| Cuvée | *Amer.* | 20 |
| Farm | *Amer.* | 25 |
| NEW Folio Enoteca | *Cal./Med.* | 23 |
| Foothill Grille | *Amer.* | 20 |
| Fumé Bistro | *Amer.* | 21 |
| In-N-Out | *Burgers* | 21 |
| Julia's | *Cal./French* | 23 |
| La Toque | *French* | 26 |
| Model Bakery | *Bakery* | 20 |
| Napa General Store | *Cal./Eclectic* | 19 |
| Napa Wine Train | *Cal.* | 17 |
| NEW Oxbow Wine | *Cal./Med.* | - |
| Pica Pica Maize | *S Amer.* | - |
| NEW Rôtisario | *BBQ* | - |
| Taylor's Auto | *Diner* | 21 |
| NEW 25º Brix | *Cal./Med.* | - |
| Ubuntu | *Cal./Vegan* | 24 |
| Uva Trattoria | *Italian* | 23 |
| Zinsvalley | *Amer.* | 20 |
| ZuZu | *Spanish* | 24 |

### RUTHERFORD

| | | |
|---|---|---|
| Auberge du Sol. | *Cal./French* | 25 |
| Rutherford Grill | *Amer.* | 23 |

## ST. HELENA

Cindy's | *Amer./Cal.* 24
Cook St. Helena | *Italian* 24
Go Fish | *Eclectic/Seafood* 23
Market | *Amer.* 22
Z Martini House | *Amer.* 26
Meadowood Grill | *Cal.* 20
Z Meadowood Rest. | *Cal.* 26
Model Bakery | *Bakery* 20
Pizzeria Tra Vigne | *Pizza* 21
Press | *Amer./Steak* 22
Taylor's Auto | *Diner* 21
Z Terra | *Amer.* 26
Tra Vigne | *Italian* 23
Wine Spectator | *Cal.* 22

## YOUNTVILLE

Z Ad Hoc | *Amer.* 26
Z Bistro Jeanty | *French* 26
Bouchon | *French* 26
Étoile | *Cal.* 25
Z French Laundry | *Amer./French* 29
Hurley's | *Cal./Med.* 17
Mustards Grill | *Amer./Cal.* 24
Napa Valley Grille | *Cal.* 20
Z Redd | *Cal.* 27

# North of San Francisco

## OCCIDENTAL

Bistro/Copains | *French* 26

# Sonoma

## BODEGA/BODEGA BAY

Duck Club | *Amer.* 20

## FORESTVILLE

Farmhouse Inn | *Cal.* 26
Mosaic | *Cal.* 26

## GEYSERVILLE

NEW Diavola | *Italian* -
Santi | *Italian* 24

## GLEN ELLEN

fig cafe | *French* 23

## GRATON

Underwood Bar | *Med.* 23
Willow Wood | *Eclectic/Med.* 23

## GUERNEVILLE

Applewood Inn | *Cal.* 24

## HEALDSBURG

Barndiva | *Amer.* 18
Bistro Ralph | *Cal./French* 22
Bovolo | *Italian* 22
Charcuterie | *French* 23
Z Cyrus | *French* 29
Downtown Bakery | *Bakery* 22
Dry Creek | *Amer.* 24
NEW Healdsburg B&G | *Amer.* -
Jimtown Store | *Deli* 18
Madrona Manor | *Amer./French* 26
Manzanita | *Cal./Med.* 20
Ravenous Cafe | *Cal./Eclectic* 22
Osake/Sake 'O | *Cal./Japanese* 23
Willi's Seafood | *Seafood* 23
Zin | *Amer.* 22

## KENWOOD

Cafe Citti | *Italian* 22
Kenwood | *Amer./French* 23

## PETALUMA

Central Market | *Cal./Med.* 23
Cucina Paradiso | *Italian* 24
Della Fattoria | *Bakery/Eclectic* 25
NEW Risibisi | *Italian* 21
Sooze Wine | *Cal.* 25
Water St. Bistro | *French* 25

## ROHNERT PARK

Z Hana Japanese | *Japanese* 26

## SANTA ROSA

Betty's Fish | *Seafood* 20
Flavor | *Cal./Eclectic* 20

Gary Chu's | *Chinese* 21
John Ash & Co. | *Cal.* 23
Monti's | *Amer./Med.* 20
Osake/Sake 'O | *Cal./Japanese* 23
Syrah | *Cal./French* 25
Willi's Wine | *Eclectic* 25
zazu | *Amer./Italian* 24

## SEBASTOPOL

NEW Hopmonk Tav. | *Eclectic* -
K&L Bistro | *French* 24
NEW Peter Lowell's | *Italian* -

## SONOMA

Z Cafe La Haye | *Amer./Cal.* 26
Carneros Bistro | *Cal.* 20
Della Santina's | *Italian* 20
Deuce | *Amer.* 22
El Dorado | *Cal./Med.* 21
girl & the fig | *French* 23
LaSalette | *Portug.* 22
Meritage Martini | *Italian* 20
Santé | *Cal./French* 24

## WINDSOR

Mirepoix | *French* 25
NEW Odyssey | *Amer.* 19

# Napa County Wineries

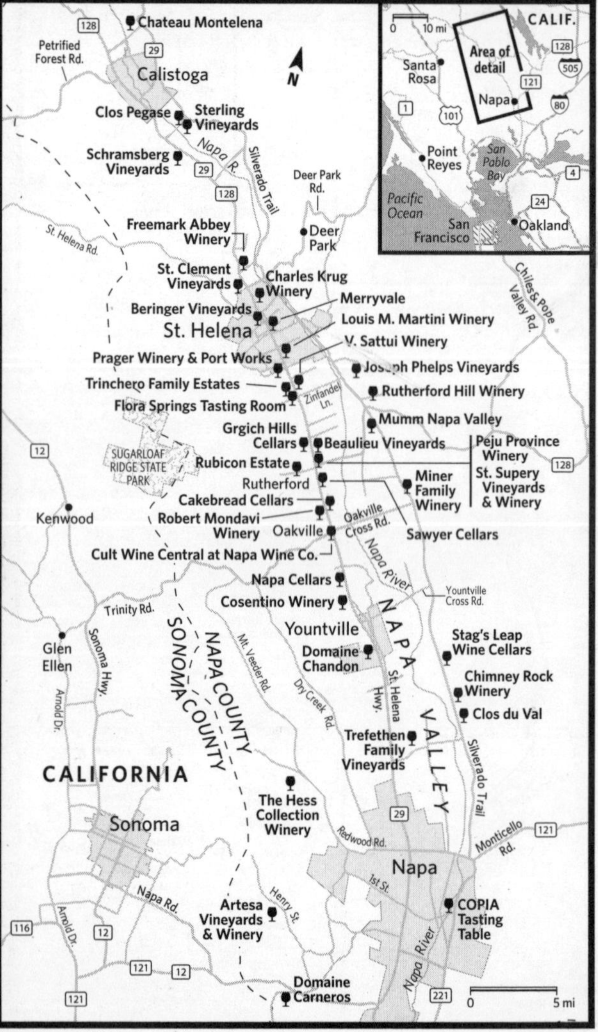

# Sonoma County Wineries

# MENDOCINO COUNTY WINERIES

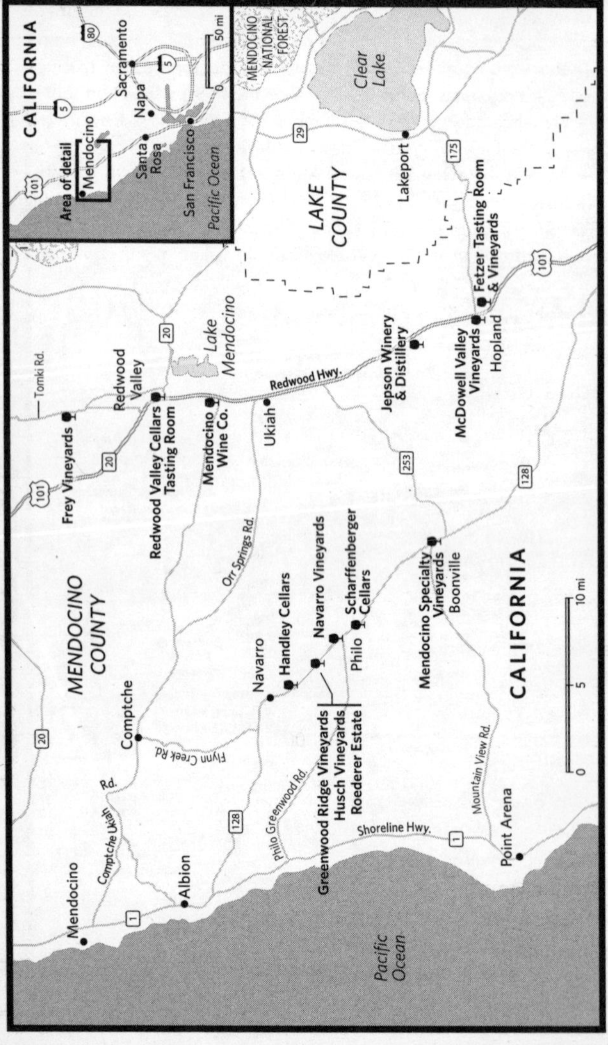

The hundreds of wineries and vineyards throughout Napa, Sonoma and Mendocino counties offer a wealth of opportunities for tastings and educational tours. Some also provide the food, wines and tables that encourage day-trippers to picnic among the vines. Check web sites or contact the wineries for details. More information can also be found at **Napa Valley Vintners Association,** (707) 963-3388, www.napavintners.com; **Sonoma Valley Vintners & Growers Alliance,** (707) 935-0803, www.sonomavalleywine.com; and **Mendocino Winegrowers Alliance,** (707) 468-9886, www.mendowine.com.

# Wineries & Vineyards

## Napa County

### Ancien Wines
4047 E. Third Ave. | Napa | 707-255-3908 | www.ancienwines.com

### Artesa Vineyards & Winery
1345 Henry Rd. | Napa | 707-224-1668 | www.artesawinery.com

### Beaulieu Vineyards
1960 St. Helena Hwy. | Rutherford | 800-264-6918 | www.bvwines.com

### Beringer Vineyards
2000 Main St. | St. Helena | 707-963-7115 | www.beringer.com

### Cakebread Cellars
8300 St. Helena Hwy. | Rutherford | 800-588-0298 | www.cakebread.com

### Charles Krug Winery
2800 Main St. | St. Helena | 707-967-2229 | 800-237-0033 | www.charleskrug.com

### Chateau Montelena
1429 Tubbs Ln. | Calistoga | 707-942-5105 | www.montelena.com

### Chimney Rock Winery
5350 Silverado Trail | Napa | 707-257-2641 | 800-257-2641 | www.chimneyrock.com

## Clos du Val
5330 Silverado Trail | Napa | 707-261-5200 | 800-993-9463 | www.closduval.com

## Clos Pegase
1060 Dunaweal Ln. | Calistoga | 707-942-4981 | 800-366-8583 | www.clospegase.com

## COPIA Tasting Table
500 First St. | Napa | 707-259-1600 | 888-512-6742 | www.copia.org

## Corison Winery
987 St. Helena Hwy. | St. Helena | 707-963-0826 | www.corison.com

## Cosentino Winery
7415 St. Helena Hwy. | Yountville | 707-944-1220 | 800-764-1220 | www.cosentinowinery.com

## Cult Wine Central at Napa Wine Co.
7830-40 St. Helena Hwy. | Oakville | 707-944-8669 | 800-848-9630 | www.cultwinecentral.com

## Cuvaison Estate Wines
4550 Silverado Trail N. | Calistoga | 707-942-2468 | www.cuvaison.com

## Domaine Carneros
1240 Duhig Rd. | Napa | 707-257-0101 | 800-716-2788 | www.domaine.com

## Domaine Chandon
1 California Dr. | Yountville | 707-944-2280 | 800-934-3975 | www.chandon.com

## Duckhorn Vineyards
1000 Lodi Ln. | St. Helena | 707-963-7108 | 888-354-8885 | www.duckhornvineyards.com

## Far Niente
1350 Acacia Dr. | Oakville | 707-944-2861 | www.farniente.com

## Flora Springs Tasting Room
677 St. Helena Hwy. S. | St. Helena | 707-967-8032 | www.florasprings.com

## Freemark Abbey Winery
3022 St. Helena Hwy. N. | St. Helena | 707-963-9694 | 800-963-9698 | www.freemarkabbey.com

## WINERIES & VINEYARDS

**Frog's Leap**
8815 Conn Creek Rd. | Rutherford | 707-963-4704 | 800-959-4704 | www.frogsleap.com

**Grgich Hills Cellars**
1829 St. Helena Hwy. | Rutherford | 707-963-2784 | 800-532-3057 | www.grgich.com

**Heitz Wine Cellars**
436 St. Helena Hwy. S. | St. Helena | 707-963-3542 | www.heitzcellar.com

**Hess Collection Winery, The**
4411 Redwood Rd. | Napa | 707-255-1144 | www.hesscollection.com

**Jocelyn Lonen Winery**
4400 Atlas Peak Rd. | Napa | 707-257-2821 | www.jocelynwines.com

**Joseph Phelps Vineyards**
200 Taplin Rd. | St. Helena | 707-963-2745 | 800-707-5789 | www.jpvwines.com

**Lagier Meredith**
4967 Dry Creek Rd. | Napa | 707-253-0653 | www.lagiermeredith.com

**Louis M. Martini Winery**
254 St. Helena Hwy. S. | St. Helena | 707-963-2736 | 800-321-9463 | www.louismartini.com

**Lynch Ranch**
1040 Main St., Suite 103 | Napa | 707-251-8822 | www.lynchvineyards.com

**Markham Vineyards**
2812 St. Helena Hwy. N. | St. Helena | 707-963-5292 | www.markhamvineyards.com

**Merryvale**
1000 Main St. | St. Helena | 707-963-7777 | 800-326-6069 | www.merryvale.com

**Miner Family Winery**
7850 Silverado Trail | Oakville | 707-944-9500 | 800-366-9463 | www.minerwines.com

**Mumm Napa Valley**
8445 Silverado Trail | Rutherford | 707-967-7700 | 800-686-6272 | www.mummcuveenapa.com

## WINERIES & VINEYARDS

### Napa Cellars
7481 St. Helena Hwy. | Oakville | 707-944-2565 | 800-535-6400 | www.napacellars.com

### Nickel & Nickel
8164 St. Helena Hwy. | Oakville | 707-967-9600 | www.nickelandnickel.com

### Peju Province Winery
8466 St. Helena Hwy. | Rutherford | 707-963-3600 | 800-446-7358 | www.peju.com

### PlumpJack Winery
620 Oakville Cross Rd. | Oakville | 707-945-1220 | www.plumpjack.com

### Prager Winery & Port Works
1281 Lewelling Ln. | St. Helena | 707-963-7678 | 800-969-7678 | www.pragerport.com

### Raymond Vineyard & Cellar
849 Zinfandel Ln. | St. Helena | 707-963-3141 | 800-525-2659 | www.raymondwine.com

### Robert Mondavi Winery
7801 St. Helena Hwy. | Oakville | 888-766-6328 | www.robertmondavi.com

### Rombauer Vineyards
3522 Silverado Trail | St. Helena | 707-963-5170 | www.rombauervineyards.com

### Rubicon Estate
1991 St. Helena Hwy. | Rutherford | 707-968-1100 | 800-782-4266 | www.rubiconestate.com

### Rutherford Hill Winery
200 Rutherford Hill Rd. | Rutherford | 707-963-1871 | 800-637-5681 | www.rutherfordhill.com

### Sawyer Cellars
8350 St. Helena Hwy. | Rutherford | 707-963-1980 | 800-818-2252 | www.sawyercellars.com

### Schramsberg Vineyards
1400 Schramsberg Rd. | Calistoga | 707-942-2414 | 800-877-3623 | www.schramsberg.com

### Silver Oak Cellars
915 Oakville Cross Rd. | Oakville | 707-944-8808 | www.silveroak.com

### Stag's Leap Wine Cellars
5766 Silverado Trail | Napa | 707-265-2441 | 866-422-7523 | www.cask23.com

### St. Clement Vineyards
2867 St. Helena Hwy. N. | St. Helena | 707-963-7221 | 800-331-8266 | www.stclement.com

### Sterling Vineyards
1111 Dunaweal Ln. | Calistoga | 707-942-3344 | 800-726-6136 | www.sterlingvineyards.com

### St. Supery Vineyards & Winery
8440 St. Helena Hwy. | Rutherford | 707-963-4507 | 800-942-0809 | www.stsupery.com

### Trefethen Family Vineyards
1160 Oak Knoll Ave. | Napa | 707-255-7700 | 866-895-7696 | www.trefethen.com

### Trinchero Family Estates
277 St. Helena Hwy. S. | St. Helena | 707-963-3104 | www.tfewines.com

### Twomey
1183 Dunaweal Ln. | Calistoga | 800-505-4850 | www.twomeycellars.com

### V. Sattui Winery
1111 White Ln. | St. Helena | 707-963-7774 | 800-799-2337 | www.vsattui.com

### ZD Wines
8383 Silverado Trail | Napa | 707-963-5188 | 800-487-7757 | www.zdwines.com

## Sonoma County

### Adler Fels Winery
5325 Corrick Ln. | Santa Rosa | 707-569-8039 | www.adlerfels.com

### Alexander Valley Vineyards
8644 Hwy. 128 | Healdsburg | 707-433-7209 | 800-888-7209 | www.avvwine.com

## WINERIES & VINEYARDS

**Amphora Wines**
4791 Dry Creek Rd. | Healdsburg | 707-431-7767 | www.amphorawines.com

**Armida Winery**
2201 Westside Rd. | Healdsburg | 707-433-2222 | www.armida.com

**Arrowood Vineyards & Winery**
14347 Sonoma Hwy. 12 | Glen Ellen | 707-935-2600 | 800-938-5170 | www.arrowoodvineyards.com

**Audelssa Estates Tasting Room**
13647 Arnold Dr. | Glen Ellen | 707-933-8514 | www.audelssa.com

**Benziger Family Winery**
1883 London Ranch Rd. | Glen Ellen | 707-935-3000 | 888-490-2739 | www.benziger.com

**B.R. Cohn Winery**
15000 Sonoma Hwy. 12 | Glen Ellen | 707-938-4064 | 800-330-4064 | www.brcohn.com

**Buena Vista Carneros**
18000 Old Winery Rd. | Sonoma | 707-938-1266 | 800-926-1266 | www.buenavistawinery.com

**California Welcome Center & Tasting Bar**
9 Fourth St. | Santa Rosa | 707-577-8674 | 800-404-7673 | www.visitsantarosa.com

**Cellar Door Tasting Room, The**
The Lodge at Sonoma, 1395 Broadway, Suite E | Sonoma | 707-938-4466 | www.sonomacellardoor.com

**Chateau St. Jean & Winery**
8555 Sonoma Hwy. 12 | Kenwood | 707-833-4134 | 800-543-7572 | www.chateaustjean.com

**Cline Cellars**
24737 Arnold Dr./Hwy. 121 | Sonoma | 707-940-4000 | 800-546-2070 | www.clinecellars.com

**Clos Du Bois Wines**
19410 Geyserville Ave. | Geyserville | 707-857-3100 | www.closdubois.com

## WINERIES & VINEYARDS

**Davis Bynum Winery**
8075 Westside Rd. | Healdsburg | 707-433-5852 | 866-442-7547 | www.davisbynum.com

**Dry Creek Vineyard**
3770 Lambert Bridge Rd. | Healdsburg | 707-433-1000 | 800-864-9463 | www.drycreekvineyard.com

**Family Wineries of Sonoma**
9200 Sonoma Hwy. 12 | Kenwood | 707-833-5504 | www.familywineries.com

**Ferrari-Carano Vineyards & Winery**
8761 Dry Creek Rd. | Healdsburg | 707-433-6700 | 800-831-0381 | www.ferrari-carano.com

**Field Stone Winery & Vineyard**
10075 Hwy. 128 | Healdsburg | 707-433-7266 | 800-544-7273 | www.fieldstonewinery.com

**Foppiano Vineyards**
12707 Old Redwood Hwy. | Healdsburg | 707-433-7272 | www.foppiano.com

**Francis Coppola's Rosso & Bianco Winery**
300 Via Archimedes | Geyserville | 707-857-1462 | www.rossobianco.com

**Gallo of Sonoma Winery**
320 Center St. | Healdsburg | 707-433-2458 | www.gallosonoma.com

**Geyser Peak Winery**
22281 Chianti Rd. | Geyserville | 707-857-9400 | 800-255-9463 | www.geyserpeakwinery.com

**Gloria Ferrer Champagne Caves**
23555 Hwy. 121 | Sonoma | 707-996-7256 | www.gloriaferrer.com

**Gundlach-Bundschu Winery**
2000 Denmark St. | Sonoma | 707-938-5277 | www.gunbun.com

**Hanna Winery**
9280 Hwy. 128 | Healdsburg | 707-431-4310 | 800-854-3987 | www.hannawinery.com

**Hop Kiln Winery**
6050 Westside Rd. | Healdsburg | 707-433-6491 | www.hopkilnwinery.com

**Imagery Estate Winery**
14335 Sonoma Hwy. 12 | Glen Ellen | 877-550-4278 | 877-550-4278 | www.imagerywinery.com

**Iron Horse Vineyards**
9786 Ross Station Rd. | Sebastopol | 707-887-1507 | www.ironhorsevineyards.com

**J. Fritz Winery**
24691 Dutcher Creek Rd. | Cloverdale | 707-894-3389 | 800-418-9643 | www.fritzwinery.com

**Jordan Vineyard & Winery**
1474 Alexander Valley Rd. | Healdsburg | 707-431-5250 | 800-654-1213 | www.jordanwinery.com

**Kendall-Jackson Wine Center**
5007 Fulton Rd. | Fulton | 707-571-8100 | 866-287-9818 | www.kj.com

**Kenwood Vineyards**
9592 Sonoma Hwy. 12 | Kenwood | 707-833-5891 | www.kenwoodvineyards.com

**Korbel Champagne Cellars**
13250 River Rd. | Guerneville | 707-824-7000 | 800-656-7235 | www.korbel.com

**Kunde Estate Winery**
9825 Sonoma Hwy. 12 | Kenwood | 707-833-5501 | www.kunde.com

**La Crema Winery**
235 Healdsburg Ave. | Healdsburg | 707-431-9400 | www.lacrema.com

**Lambert Bridge Winery**
4085 W. Dry Creek Rd. | Healdsburg | 707-431-9600 | 800-975-0555 | www.lambertbridge.com

**Landmark Vineyards**
101 Adobe Canyon Rd. | Kenwood | 707-833-0053 | 800-452-6365 | www.landmarkwine.com

**Ledson Winery**
7335 Sonoma Hwy. 12 | Kenwood | 707-537-3810 | www.ledson.com

**Locals: A Collective Tasting Room**
21023A Geyserville Ave. | Geyserville | 707-857-4900 | www.tastelocalwines.com

**Matanzas Creek Winery**
6097 Bennett Valley Rd. | Santa Rosa | 707-528-6464 | 800-590-6464 | www.matanzascreek.com

**Michel-Schlumberger Wines**
4155 Wine Creek Rd. | Healdsburg | 707-433-7427 | www.michelschlumberger.com

**Murphy-Goode Winery**
20 Matheson St. | Healdsburg | 800-444-7644 | www.murphygoodewinery.com

**Pedroncelli Winery**
1220 Canyon Rd. | Geyserville | 707-857-3531 | 800-836-3894 | www.pedroncelli.com

**Ravenswood Winery**
18701 Gehricke Rd. | Sonoma | 707-933-2332 | 888-669-4679 | www.ravenswood-wine.com

**Robert Young Estate**
4960 Red Winery Rd. | Geyserville | 707-431-4811 | www.ryew.com

**Rodney Strong Vineyards**
11455 Old Redwood Hwy. | Healdsburg | 707-431-1533 | 800-678-4763 | www.rodneystrong.com

**Rosenblum Cellars**
250 Center St. | Healdsburg | 707-431-1169 | www.rosenblumcellars.com

**Sable Ridge Vineyards**
6320 Jamison Rd. | Santa Rosa | 707-542-3138 | www.sableridge.com

**Schug Carneros Estate**
602 Bonneau Rd. | Sonoma | 707-939-9363 | 800-966-9365 | www.schugwinery.com

**Sebastiani Vineyards**
389 Fourth St. E. | Sonoma | 707-933-3230 | 800-888-5532 | www.sebastiani.com

**Simi Winery**
16275 Healdsburg Ave. | Healdsburg | 707-433-6981 | 800-746-4880 | www.simiwinery.com

**St. Francis Vineyard & Winery**
100 Pythian Rd. | Santa Rosa | 707-833-0242 | 888-675-9463 | www.stfranciswine.com

**Stuhlmuller Vineyards**
4951 West Soda Rock Ln. | Geyserville | 707-431-7099 | www.stuhlmullervineyards.com

**Tin Barn Vineyards**
21692 Eighth St. E., Suite 340 | Sonoma | 707-938-5430 | www.tinbarnvineyards.com

**Trentadue Winery & Vineyards**
19170 Geyserville Ave. | Geyserville | 707-433-3104 | 888-332-3032 | www.trentadue.com

**Valley of the Moon Winery**
777 Madrone Rd. | Glen Ellen | 707-996-6941 | www.valleyofthemoonwinery.com

**Viansa Winery & Italian Marketplace**
25200 Arnold Dr. | Sonoma | 800-995-4740 | www.viansa.com

**Wattle Creek Winery**
25510 River Rd. | Cloverdale | 707-894-5166 | www.wattlecreek.com

**White Oak Vineyards**
7505 Hwy. 128 | Healdsburg | 707-433-8429 | www.whiteoakwinery.com

**Wine Room, The**
9575 Sonoma Hwy. 12 | Kenwood | 707-833-6131 | www.the-wine-room.com

## Mendocino County

**Fetzer Vineyards Tasting Room**
12901 Old River Rd. | Hopland | 707-744-1250 | 800-846-8637 | www.fetzer.com

**Frey Vineyards**
14000 Tomki Rd. | Redwood Valley | 707-485-5177 | 800-760-3739 | www.freywine.com

## WINERIES & VINEYARDS

**Greenwood Ridge Vineyards**
5501 Hwy. 128 | Philo | 707-895-2002 | www.greenwoodridge.com

**Handley Cellars**
3151 Hwy. 128 | Philo | 707-895-3876 | 800-733-3151 | www.handleycellars.com

**Husch Vineyards**
4400 Hwy. 128 | Philo | 707-895-3216 | 800-554-8724 | www.huschvineyards.com

**Jepson Winery & Distillery**
10400 S. Hwy. 101 | Ukiah | 707-468-8936 | 800-516-7342 | www.jepsonwine.com

**McDowell Valley Vineyards**
13380 South Hwy. 101 | Hopland | 707-744-8911 | www.mcdowellsyrah.com

**Mendocino Specialty Vineyards**
17810 Farrer Ln. | Boonville | 707-895-3993

**Mendocino Wine Co.**
501 Parducci Rd. | Ukiah | 707-463-5350 | 888-362-9463 | www.mendocinowineco.com

**Navarro Vineyards**
5601 Hwy. 128 | Philo | 707-895-3686 | 800-537-9463 | www.navarrowine.com

**Redwood Valley Cellars Tasting Room**
7051 N. State St. | Redwood Valley | 707-485-0322 | www.redwoodvalleycellars.com

**Roederer Estate**
4501 Hwy. 128 | Philo | 707-895-2288 | www.roedererestate.com

**Scharffenberger Cellars**
8501 Hwy. 128 | Philo | 707-895-2957 | www.scharffenbergercellars.com

# Wine Vintage Chart

This chart (prepared by University of South Carolina law professor **Howard Stravitz,** and based on our 0 to 30 ratings scale) reflects the vintage quality and the wine's readiness to drink.

| Whites | 88 | 89 | 90 | 94 | 95 | 96 | 97 | 98 | 99 | 00 | 01 | 02 | 03 | 04 | 05 | 06 |
|---|---|---|---|---|---|---|---|---|---|---|---|---|---|---|---|---|
| **French:** | | | | | | | | | | | | | | | | |
| Alsace | - | 25 | 25 | 24 | 23 | 23 | 22 | 25 | 23 | 25 | 27 | 25 | 22 | 24 | 25 | - |
| Burgundy | - | 23 | 22 | - | 28 | 27 | 24 | 22 | 26 | 25 | 24 | 27 | 23 | 27 | 26 | 24 |
| Loire Valley | - | - | - | - | - | - | - | - | - | 24 | 25 | 26 | 23 | 24 | 27 | 24 |
| **California:** | | | | | | | | | | | | | | | | |
| Chardonnay | - | - | - | - | - | - | - | - | 24 | 23 | 26 | 26 | 25 | 27 | 29 | 25 |
| Sauvignon Blanc | - | - | - | - | - | - | - | - | - | - | 27 | 28 | 26 | 27 | 26 | 27 |
| **German:** | 25 | 26 | 27 | 24 | 23 | 26 | 25 | 26 | 23 | 21 | 29 | 27 | 24 | 26 | 28 | - |

| Reds | 88 | 89 | 90 | 94 | 95 | 96 | 97 | 98 | 99 | 00 | 01 | 02 | 03 | 04 | 05 | 86 |
|---|---|---|---|---|---|---|---|---|---|---|---|---|---|---|---|---|
| **French:** | | | | | | | | | | | | | | | | |
| Bordeaux | 23 | 25 | 29 | 22 | 26 | 25 | 23 | 25 | 24 | 29 | 26 | 24 | 25 | 24 | 27 | 25 |
| Burgundy | - | 24 | 26 | - | 26 | 27 | 25 | 22 | 27 | 22 | 24 | 27 | 25 | 25 | 27 | 25 |
| Rhône | 26 | 28 | 28 | 24 | 26 | 22 | 25 | 27 | 26 | 27 | 26 | - | 25 | 24 | 25 | - |
| **California:** | | | | | | | | | | | | | | | | |
| Cab./Merlot | - | - | 28 | 29 | 27 | 25 | 28 | 23 | 26 | 22 | 27 | 26 | 25 | 24 | 24 | 23 |
| Pinot Noir | - | - | - | - | - | - | 24 | 23 | 24 | 23 | 27 | 28 | 26 | 25 | 24 | - |
| Zinfandel | - | - | - | - | - | - | - | - | - | - | 25 | 23 | 27 | 24 | 23 | - |
| **Oregon:** | | | | | | | | | | | | | | | | |
| Pinot Noir | - | - | - | - | - | - | - | - | - | - | - | 27 | 25 | 26 | 27 | - |
| **Italian:** | | | | | | | | | | | | | | | | |
| Tuscany | - | - | 25 | 22 | 24 | 20 | 29 | 24 | 27 | 24 | 27 | 20 | 25 | 25 | 22 | 24 |
| Piedmont | - | 27 | 27 | - | 23 | 26 | 27 | 26 | 25 | 28 | 27 | 20 | 24 | 25 | 26 | - |
| **Spanish:** | | | | | | | | | | | | | | | | |
| Rioja | - | - | - | 26 | 26 | 24 | 25 | 22 | 25 | 24 | 27 | 20 | 24 | 25 | 26 | 24 |
| **Australian:** | | | | | | | | | | | | | | | | |
| Shiraz/Cab. | - | - | - | 24 | 26 | 23 | 26 | 28 | 24 | 24 | 27 | 27 | 25 | 26 | 24 | - |